AMAZING ADVENTURES IN HEARING GOD'S VOICE

INTIMATE AND EFFORTLESS CONVERSATIONS WITH YOUR CREATOR ARE EASIER THAN YOU THINK!

RINDA HO

CONTENTS

Thank You For Buying My Book!	vii
Foreword	xiii
Preface	xvii
Introduction	xxi
1. Why Does God Want To Speak To Me?	1
2. Who Does God Want To Speak To?	23
3. When Does God Speak To You?	43
4. Where Does God Speak To You?	61
5. What Does God Want to Speak to You About?	69
6. How Does God Speak To You?	105
7. How Does God Use Your Five Spiritual Senses to Speak to You?	127
8. What Do You Do With What You Have Heard From God?	153
9. Potential Hindrances In Hearing God's Voice	173
Conclusion	195
Thank You	197
Testimonies from Christians who have learned to hear God's voice	199
Please Share	211
About the Author	213

Amazing Adventures in Hearing God's Voice

Copyright © 2020 by Rinda Ho

All right reserved. This book is protected by the copyright laws of the United States of America, Australia, the United Kingdom, and Canada. No part of this publication may be reproduced, stored in a retrieval system, or transmitted in any form or by any means – electronic, mechanical, photocopy, recording, or any other – except for brief quotations, without the prior permission of the author.

Unless otherwise noted, all Scripture references are taken from the NEW INTERNATIONAL VERSION. Copyright ©1973, 1978, 1984 International Bible Society. Used by permission of Zondervan Bible Publishers.

Ebook ISBN 13: 978-0-6487347-1-0

Paperback ISBN 13: 978-0-6487347-0-3

Hardback ISBN 13: 978-0-6487347-2-7

Cover design: 100 Covers (100covers.com)

Proofreaders: Graham and Dianne Storey, Cynthia Tan

This book is dedicated to:

- My heavenly Father, who commissioned me to write this book and who took the first move to communicate with me.

- Jesus Christ, my Lord, who made me righteous so that I can come boldly before God's throne room at any time.

- The Holy Spirit who reveals the Father's heart to me and longs to converse with all His children.

- My loving husband, Paul, who has encouraged me and supported me each step of the way to finish writing this book.

- My loving son, Ben, and my daughter-in-law, Andrea, for cheering me on.

- My eldest brother, Charles Tan, who went home to be with the Lord on June 11, 2016.

- My loving mum, Chua Yong Siew, who slipped into eternity on September 15, 2019.

- Every reader of this book, whose pursuit to hear God's voice will be the most rewarding adventure that they will ever embark on.

THANK YOU FOR BUYING MY BOOK!

First of all, thank you for purchasing this book: *Amazing Adventures in Hearing God's Voice*. I know you could have picked any number of books to read, but you picked this book and for that, I am extremely grateful.

As a token of appreciation, I would like to give you two free gifts:

1. A free workbook for you to write what God is saying to you during the activation exercises. (Get it here: https://www.subscribepage.com/j7k6m5.)
2. The free ebook, *10 Questions You May Have about Hearing God's Voice*. (Get it here: https://www.subscribepage.com/j7k6m5_copy.)

I hope that reading the book helps you embark on the amazing adventure of hearing God's voice. If so, I would be most grateful if you could share this book with your friends and family by posting on Facebook and Twitter.

ENDORSEMENTS

"Jesus Christ, the Son of God, was able to establish His Kingdom on this earth 2000 years ago only because He was constantly seeking and hearing the voice of the Father. '*I can of Myself do nothing. As I hear, I perform*' (John 5:30). God can do greater wonders through you even as you grow to hear His voice every day. It's not a choice. It's a lifestyle of those who follow Him. This book will equip you to hear His voice."

—Evangelist Kiran Murali, Jesus is Alive Ministries (Chennai, India)

"This is an insightful and practical book for anyone desiring to hear God's voice speaking to them daily and yet in a natural way without fear that it would deviate from God's word, plans, and will. I particularly enjoyed the simple way in which each step is conveyed and all the time pointing to Christ and His glory as the ultimate goal of hearing God."

—Thomas Lim, Missions Pastor, Agape Baptist Church (Singapore)

"*My sheep listen to My voice; I know them, and they follow Me* (John 10:27). God is a communicative God who speaks to us all the time. The issue is whether we know how to tune in. Drawing from years of personal experience, this book is a practical and powerful resource for every Christian who desires to recognize and follow God's voice. Experience a new level of intimacy with God as you remove every hindrance, activate your spiritual senses, and converse with Him like never before. Dare to believe that your faith life will never be the same again!"

—Reverend Dominic Yeo, General Superintendent, The Assemblies of God of Singapore. Lead Pastor, Trinity Christian Centre (Singapore), Author of *Potential to Fulfillment*

"Throughout the more than twenty years that I have known Rinda, I have found her to have a heart that is constantly inclined towards her Lord. She delights to hear the Holy Spirit's gentle whisper and often wakes up in the early hours of the morning to incline her ear to hear what her Lord has for her. This book is a testimony to the rich gems that have been her experience and I am sure this book will encourage many of you to purposefully set aside more time for worship and prayer so that you too may hear these words of the Lord, 'Whether you turn to the right or the left, your ears will hear a voice behind you, saying, "This is the way; walk in it' (Isaiah 30:21)."

—**Lim Cheng Lai, Founding Pastor, Faith Community Church (Perth, Western Australia)**

"The book is an easy read and I love the practical way in which it has been written. Thank you for simplifying the process of hearing God's voice. You have helped remove years of complexity that fear and ignorance has built up. The activities at the end of each chapter assist the reader to apply what was learned so that knowledge becomes a heart experience. I also love the way you present a well-balanced account of Scripture. I believe this book will certainly help many people draw closer to the Lord. A greater level of intimacy awaits the reader."

—**Joel Chelliah, Senior Pastor, Centrepoint Church (Perth, Western Australia); State President of the Assemblies of God in Australia; National Director of Harvestnet Australia, Author of *The Chat: Understanding puberty, pornography, sex, and marriage***

"There is a wealth of intrigue in Rinda's masterpiece, *Amazing Adventures in Hearing God's Voice*. Her life and book portray plainly the ease and possibility of having an effortless and secure relationship with our God! This book will inspire you and cause you to really know Him and His wonderful and yet simple unique ways He relates to you. This is a must-read if you are looking for answers on this topic. You will be graced by the Father, leading you gently and intimately in union with Him. I can confidently say you will hear His Voice and converse with

Papa at rest and ease through this book. Whether you turn to the right or to the left, your ears will hear a voice behind you, saying, 'This is the way; walk in it' (Isaiah 30:21)."

—Esther Madeline Yan-Teo, Founder, Kingdom Glory International, Co-Pastor, Church of Living Water; (Perth, Western Australia), Spirit-led worship artist/songwriter (CDs: Jesus Kingdom Glory; Jesus the Gateway; Spirit of Glory)

"Fresh perspectives keep popping up at every page. The more you read the more you grow to know the Lord's love for you. You'll want to try out the activation exercises; it's so easy to hear from our Heavenly Father. Being prophetic is not for the elite, it's for the ordinary believer. Every myth demystified."

—Sabrina Chow, Senior Pastor, Risen Christian Assembly (Singapore)

"This book makes hearing God's voice simple and doable for anyone who desires intimacy with God. Rinda writes from her own adventure in learning to hear from God. In a simple manner, she articulates her Bible-based beliefs about hearing God's voice today and some hindrances that may be encountered. Christians stepping into the adventure of hearing God's voice will find the activation exercises at the end of each chapter helpful."

—Reverend Anita Chia, Assembly of God minister (Singapore)

"Rinda has successfully given a well-researched and comprehensive topic of how to hear from God with practical applications and testimonies. A very helpful book for the novice and those who have a deeper desire to want to hear from God. You will be blessed and encouraged when you read this book."

—Pastors David & Jacey Lee, Founders and Directors of the House of Shalom ministry (England)

"God wants to speak to His people and to guide and fill them with great joy. However, they tend to forget how to listen to Him and for that, this book is the answer. Enjoy reading this book as well as discovering the amazing adventures of hearing God's voice that will guide and bring great enjoyment in your journey of life."

—Nynto Piojo, Senior Pastor, Voice of Truth (Iloilo, Philippines)

"This book gives the answers and solution to many queries on how to listen to and communicate with God, believers and unbelievers alike, for God desires that all will come to the saving knowledge of Jesus Christ. It is simple and easy to follow and understand and very practical. It is biblically sound, and it edifies, encourages, and comforts. As iron sharpens iron, so this book will help you sharpen your spiritual senses and make you sensitive to the things of God. It will help you to strategically walk in the supernatural as sons of God led by God's Spirit to fulfill His Divine purpose in your generation. I highly recommend this book as a manual for prophetic students of this generation."

—Pastor Ruben Pamplona, God is Good Church (Iloilo, Philippines)

"The reader will be updated and upgraded beyond your imagination in your prophetic walk as you read this book. The reader will fulfill their prophetic destiny as they let God activate their supernatural senses. You will soar high like an eagle beyond your boundary."

—Pastor Philip Ng, God is Good Church (Iloilo, Philippines)

FOREWORD

My heart is thrilled to read Rinda Ho's incredible book, *Amazing Adventures in Hearing God's Voice*. As her Senior Pastor while she and her husband lived in Singapore, it is so exciting and rewarding to witness how her spiritual hunger and growth have produced such an important book for the Body of Christ.

The prophetic is something greatly neglected and yet critically needed in our churches today. Scripture clearly teaches us that everyone should prophesy. However, that does not make us all prophets. Yet, the Apostle Paul clearly outlined in 1 Corinthians 12-14, the importance of this ministry through and to the Body of Christ. However, fear of abuse and the lack of proper teaching in this area of the church life have created a big, empty vacuum in our churches and in the lives of many believers. Could it be that we ourselves are not hearing from God and thus do not know how to lead our people into this relationship with God?

Friends, this book could be the answer you have been needing. It is a wonderfully simple, Biblically accurate, profoundly encouraging, and Christ-honouring tool to help guide you and others into a new intimate walk with the Lord.

I love the fact that it is an easy and practical reading. It shows how hearing from God is not complicated. It is easy because God desires to speak to those who are listening. Therefore, you are quickly drawn into a closer and more intimate relationship with Jesus, our Lord, and Saviour.

Rinda not only sought God, but also searched until she found help for her own spiritual answers concerning how she could hear from God. She chased after God's heart and thankfully found the help and guidance she needed to enable her to not only hear God personally, but also to equip her to train and empower many others.

In this book, her desire to know and hear from God begins to grip your heart and spirit to dare and believe that you too can hear regularly from God. All the mystic is blown away and the true reality of God's voice and presence becomes real to you personally.

However, she does not leave you hanging, for she has provided very helpful activation exercises at the end of each chapter. Step by step you will make progress into a new level of hearing accurately from God. This will thrill your heart and awaken a new and fresh desire to spend more time with the Lord and to know Him and understand His heart for His people.

Another important aspect of this incredible book is the fact that it is based on Scripture. Rinda is always pointing the readers to Jesus and His love and desire to be an intimate part of their daily lives, not just in church, but in every area of their lives, family or business. God can and will speak to you in every arena of your daily life.

As a pastor who does a lot of training and consultation in churches all around the world, I find this book a definite "must-have, must-read, must use" book for every believer. I encourage pastors to buy and give this book to every member of their church. Ask God for a trained and anointed leader, establish your protocols, and get this ministry activated in your church. This book is a practical and powerful resource for training a new prophetic generation. God knew we needed it.

—**Reverend Dr. Naomi Dowdy**

Pastor, Trainer, Consultant, Author

Founder Chancellor, Theological Centre of Asia (TCA) College, Singapore

Former Senior Pastor, Trinity Christian Centre, Singapore

Author of 6 books:

1. Strength to stand: Equipping the church for impact through Apostolic-Prophetic leadership

2. Moving on and moving up -10 practical principles for getting to the next level

3. Moving on and moving up from succession to significance

4. Moving on and moving up in the marketplace

5. Commissioning modern day apostles

6. Destiny calling—Your beginning does not determine your end

https://www.Naomidowdy.com

PREFACE

Why I Wrote This Book

For many years, it has been my great desire (as I am sure it is for many of you reading this book) to be able to hear God's voice with clarity and consistency. I have personally bought many books and read many articles on how to hear God's voice. There was a sense of excitement and anticipation that finally, I am going to learn the "secret." Many of the books I read gave accounts of the author's amazing journey in hearing God's voice. However, as I read each chapter in anticipation, I was disappointed many times, even after reading the last page, that I hadn't learned the "how" yet. Many authors told me how they did it and implied that I could do it as well, but sadly did not give me a step-by-step process. My question was: "How about me? Can someone *please* show me or tell me how to do it, too?"

Thus began my journey of finding out whether an ordinary person like you and me are able to hear God's voice consistently and accurately. And if this is at all possible, then how is it done? I used to think that since there was so much "secrecy" about this topic, then it must be extremely difficult for an "ordinary" Christian to learn how to hear and speak to God. I imagined that I had to enroll in the School of the

Holy Spirit to help me learn this very important skill. It was a long journey as I did not have a mentor. However, God eventually led me to the Father's Heart Ministry by Russell Walden, where I joined his online prophetic mentoring training program. Suddenly, like a series of lightbulb moments, it all made sense to me. Russell helped me understand the step-by-step foundation of hearing God's voice which I had been so desperate to master. Prior to graduating, I was required to teach a group about how to hear His voice. This experience ignited a passion within me to teach other people what I had learned about hearing the voice of God and to simplify the process for them.

After many years of teaching groups of people how to hear God's voice, I received a mandate from God to write this book in order to help many more people hear His voice, beyond simply those who were able to attend my training class. I am excited to share with you this step-by-step, hands-on activation to experience hearing God's voice for yourself. You do not need to depend on your ability to hear His voice but His ability to teach you how.

I am looking forward to being used by God to activate the ability within each reader to hear the voice of the Father (through the Holy Spirit) for themselves and for others through practicing to listen to Him in a safe environment. You can stand on my shoulders and glean from my learnings so that you can go further and higher than me, because now you have this book as a manual. It's a book I wish I'd had all those years ago. You will bring the heavenly Father so much pleasure when you can have conversations with him *anytime*, *anywhere* and about *anything*.

Why You Should Read This Book

This book will help you answer questions you may be too afraid to ask about hearing God's voice. It is not a topic that is preached on very often in churches and many people may not have time to answer your questions, which you might fear sound "silly" or "obvious." It's even more difficult when you have been a Christian for a long time, and it's expected that you should already know how to hear God's voice.

This book covers the why, who, where, when, and most importantly, the how. Each chapter has activation exercises that give you the opportunity to practice what you have just learned. You will be surprised at how easy it is, because God will make the first move and make it easy for you to connect with Him.

The benefits of you learning to hear God's voice, to name just a few, are:

- It brings blessing to your life
- It helps you to see yourself, others, and your situation more clearly
- It helps you know His will and plan for every area of your life (e.g. career, ministry, life partner, marriage, relationship, etc.)
- You will learn how to pray specifically for loved ones and friends' salvation

Come on, take the challenge and begin the exhilarating and amazing adventures of hearing His voice every day and getting answers for every area of your life!

INTRODUCTION

Why the title *Amazing Adventures in Hearing God's Voice?* Because it is so exciting to hear His voice, especially for those who haven't learned how to hear His voice before. Imagine being able to have a conversation with Him. No more boring one-sided prayer. No more feeling like your prayer has hit the ceiling and bounced back to you, leaving you worried, sad, frustrated, and angry. At such times, have you ever raised your fist at God and demanded, "Where are You? Are You listening to me? Don't You care about me and what I am going through? If you have ever been in such a situation (which I am sure many of us have), then this book is for you.

This book will show you step-by-step how to converse/talk with God and hear Him responding back to you. I know some of you are asking whether this is at all possible. I have met many people who desire to hear His voice, but after reading so many books on this topic, have come to the sad conclusion that hearing His voice is just too hard. They decide to either leave it to the elite few who have this "gift," or seek someone with the prophetic gift to give them a prophetic word instead of learning to listen to God directly. This is very much like the children of Israel in the Bible who told Moses: "Speak to God and let us know what He says. We are too afraid of Him (Exodus 20:19)." Isn't it great that, because of Jesus, all of us can now come boldly to His throne room to receive help in times of need and that we do not need to go through someone else?

This book is simple to read because it is written by an ordinary Christian. You don't need theological knowledge to understand the simple truth that God wants to communicate with you and that you can communicate with Him, too. There is no exception and no exemption on with whom God communicates. "My sheep hear My voice" will be a reality to you 24/7 (John 10:27).

This book is for anyone who is willing to let go of doubt, fear, and unbelief and take the step of faith to let the Holy Spirit reveal the truth that you can hear God's voice.

For you who may find it difficult to believe that God can use your imagination to speak to you or who hold the wrong belief that you need to earn the right to hear God's voice, I pray that this book will help remove these hindrances so that you too can hear His voice.

I have created a workbook especially for you so that you can use it to journal your conversations with your heavenly Father. You can download the workbook here: https://www.subscribepage.com/j7k6m5

God is a person, not a machine. He longs for fellowship.
—*Bill Johnson, Hosting the presence every day*

I

WHY DOES GOD WANT TO SPEAK TO ME?

Do you have an innate desire to connect with God and with each other? God is more eager to connect with you than you could possibly imagine. People from various religions try to find God. For example, when you walk into various temples, you will notice many idols of gods. Devotees of all religions attempt to reach out to a god that they can physically touch. Sadly, these man-made idols do not have the power or the ability to help or comfort them in their time of need because they have eyes that cannot see, ears that cannot hear, and hands that cannot reach out to them.

We all love this desire to connect with people, and that is the reason why social media such as Facebook, Twitter, WhatsApp, FaceTime, and LinkedIn are so popular. There are even some people who boast of having one million friends on Facebook. Why do we have this insatiable desire to be part of a group, even if we hardly know its members? To say that we have so many friends on Facebook makes us feel wanted, accepted, and recognized. We all have a need to feel validated.

Why does God want to speak with me even though He knows that I am imperfect?

Do you wonder why the Creator of the universe, the all-powerful God, wants to converse with you? Doesn't God know that you have sin in your life? You may even struggle to connect among your circle of close friends. How about your feelings of being vulnerable, depressed, or suicidal? How about times when you feel angry and frustrated? Why on earth does God want to speak with you when you sometimes don't even like yourself? At least on Facebook or Twitter, you can show your "good side," which you want people to see. Since God is all-knowing, He knows when you aren't living a holy life. You may also struggle with low self-worth regarding the imperfections in your body, face, speech, etc. Is He sure that He wants to speak with you? You most probably do not think so, therefore you hide or run away from Him rather than speak or have anything to do with Him.

Listed below are some reasons God wants to speak to you.

1. He created you

He wants to speak to you because He created and treasures you. Let me give you an illustration. Have you ever seen a child doing his first drawing or building something with Legos for the first time? Even though it may not look much like what he says it is, he feels proud that he has created something. In the child's mind, he already sees the end product. If you try to multiply that feeling of pride and joy a million times, maybe you can begin to fathom a tiny bit of how God felt when He created you. When He created you, He put good and perfect gifts inside you. He dreamed about how you would look when He had finished creating you. The Bible says that *"we are God's workmanship created in Christ Jesus to do good works, which God prepared in advance for us to do"* (Ephesians 2:10). Even the Mona Lisa or the most beautiful picture cannot compare to your beauty and uniqueness in God's eyes. You have been wonderfully created by a loving heavenly Father.

2. He is interested in you

Many Christians and non-Christians cannot believe that there is a God in this universe who is interested in them to such an extent that He wants to personally speak with them. It is a belief that not only permeates adults but teenagers and children as well. In many cultures, females are not permitted to speak in front of males, and children are told that they are to be seen and not heard. Therefore, it is not surprising that this warped belief is still prevalent today. As the family unit breaks down, and we use more and more electronic devices to communicate, the less we *truly* communicate with each other. Even parents hardly communicate with their own children nowadays. It's quite common to see parents and children using their mobile phones and not engaging in a face-to-face conversation with each other in a restaurant.

Communication among married couples is becoming less due to the pressures of daily life. It is the norm for married couples to relax in front of the television during dinner. They talk about television programs instead of what is going on in each other's lives. Even among children, it is not uncommon to see them in a social gathering engaging with some sort of electronic device instead of interacting with each other. The scary thing is that parents are permitting children as young as two years old to be entertained with some sort of electronic device. Even in the work environment, the use of email is the primary mode of communication and workmates seldom venture out of their work area to talk to each other.

We are so used to the norm of only communicating through electronic means, that it is beyond our comprehension that the God who created the universe is interested enough to want to speak to us. Most of us can only dream of our prayers being answered by Him if we are "lucky" or "holy" enough. If God tells you that He not only listens to your prayers but wants to have a conversation with you, it may sound impossible and incomprehensible to your mere human thinking. To be told that He wants to converse with you, not because He "has to" but because He "wants to" blows your understanding out of the window.

We all want to reach out to God and have divine revelation concerning our lives. When I was a young girl, my mom brought me to various Chinese temples where many statues of gods were housed. I was afraid to go inside the temple because I found some of the faces of the statues very scary and fierce-looking. In my mind, I imagined that God would have a kind and loving face. Looking back, even when I was young, my heavenly Father had already marked me to know Him. He wanted to reveal Himself to me as my kind heavenly Father who can help me when I pray to Him in time of need. Not only that, but He also wants to have an intimate relationship with me!

3. He wants you to know His character

Many of you reading this book are probably asking, "If there are so many gods and so many voices that I hear, how can I ever know which is God's voice?" One of the obvious ways to know God's voice is through the Bible because the Bible reveals to you the voice of God and His character. As you begin to know Him through the Bible, you will know God's character. This will, in turn, help you start to discern His voice from the myriad of voices that you hear daily shouting for your attention. Hearing God's voice has less to do with how it sounds and more to do with the character of God. The Bible reveals to you that God's character never changes through the ages. His faithfulness, love, kindness, and patience will never change. God's words do not change, and when you focus on discovering the character of God through the Bible, you will begin to discern His voice, not only through Scripture, but also through the other ways He speaks.

4. He wants to speak to you through the Bible and also through other means

Many Christians have been taught that the Bible is the *only* way God speaks to them. While the Bible is a very important and valuable avenue for communicating with God, it must be read in connection with other ways that God may choose to speak to you. He can speak to you through dreams, visions, circumstances, and even through His creation. Many Christians read the Bible each day but still don't know how to get answers for their lives. No wonder many of us grow up disillusioned and feel disconnected from God. There is no way that you can have real fellowship and relationship with God when you utilize this one-way communication with Him. God speaks to you through so many ways which are not limited to just the Bible.

5. He longs for a relationship and desires daily conversations with you

Jesus died so that He could re-establish your relationship with your heavenly Father. How can you have a relationship with Him if you don't speak to Him or He doesn't speak to you? If you speak to God and He does not respond to you, then it's no different from talking to some man-made idols that are handcrafted by a human being.

Ryan Watt in his book, *School of the Supernatural: Live the Supernatural Life That God Created You to Live*, wrote:

> *Every single person should be able to hear God's voice. He is our Bridegroom. How many brides and bridegrooms do you know who don't talk daily? How many people in an intense love relationship do not talk daily or at least every other day?*

Lyn Packer in her book, *Releasing Heaven into Earth*, made this observation:

> *It's in dialogue that we get to know someone's heart and what they are really like. True relationship is a progressive journey of self-disclosure by both parties in that relationship. It's in this place of dialogue that we get to understand what God wants—His plans and purposes—and because we've taken the time to get to know Him, we can know His heart as well as His plans and purposes.*

In their book, *The Voice of God*, Scott Stanley, and Brandon Wood wrote:

> *I was getting to a point where I began thinking that God no longer speaks to most people. I even rationalized that He may have been so busy facilitating things in my life that He didn't have time to talk or explain things to me. Yet, I still had a nagging thought: "What kind of father would I be if I didn't talk to my children?" I knew the answer would be a "bad" father, but I also knew, with everything that had happened recently in my life, that God is an amazing Father. So why*

wasn't He talking to me or, if He was, why couldn't I hear Him speak?

The late Kim Clement in his book, *Call Me Crazy, But I'm Hearing God's Voice: Secrets to Hearing the Voice of God,* explained:

> *The one thing that we've failed to understand is that God created man for one main reason—friendship. During His earthly ministry, Christ said these words to His disciples, "No longer do I call you servants, but I have called you friends" (John 15: 15). The word used for friends in the Greek is "Philos" or "Philogos," which means "someone to talk to" or "someone close to talk to." God created you and me to talk to. He's not the problem, we are. He never ran from Adam and Eve, they ran from Him because of their perception of Him. People in general, are hungry to hear God speak to them. They've heard interpretations of His Word and would like to find out for themselves. Once you understand the "friendship" aspect of your relationship with God, you will easily hear Him when He whispers or speaks audibly.*

6. He wants to teach you to recognize His voice

Many people have the misconception that hearing God's voice is a mystery and that He is like the wind that blows where it wishes. They may be able to hear the sound of the wind, but they cannot tell where it comes from or where it is going (John 3:5). In 1 Kings 19:11, it is written: *"But the Lord was not in the wind."* He wants you to respond to Him when He speaks so He can have a dialogue with you. As you do this, you will begin to experience the amazing and exciting Christian lifestyle of continual conversing with Him. God is not trying to be mysterious or make it difficult for you to find Him. Instead, He is trying to make His communication clear to you so that you can hear Him clearly and consistently all the time.

You live in a world where there are many voices trying to get your attention. When you face a certain situation, the voice of your emotions, reasoning, your upbringing, and your own experience may cloud your ability to discern the voice of God. Other voices, such as the voices of your culture, the media, and the expectation of other people may also hinder you from hearing His voice clearly. The good news is that you don't need to rely on your ability to hear God's voice, but you can instead rely on His ability to use every way and means to communicate with you. He will not give up on you when you don't respond to a particular way of communication, but He might change to another mode since He's not limited by your finite ways of communication. The more you are open to the various ways that He can speak to you, the more opportunity you give Him and yourself to hear Him clearly and regularly.

Why do you need to hear God's voice?

You may question the need to hear God's voice as you may have been taught to be self-sufficient and to not depend on or trust anyone (including God who is "up there somewhere"). There is a perception that you are doing fine without God anyway, so why bother going through the pain of learning to hear His voice? Why do you need to hear His voice when you may already be having difficulties in connecting with your own parents and friends whom you can see, hear, and touch?

Below are some reasons why you need to hear God's voice:

1. So He can fill the vacuum inside you

God created a vacuum inside of you when He created you. Only *He* can fill that vacuum, so that you can feel loved, significant, and fulfilled. Many believe they can achieve great things without any need to have God in their lives. However, all their successes will come to nothing or even destroy them if they do not have a relationship with God. Think of all the film stars, rock stars, and celebrities who have achieved fame and money but who have ended up destroying their lives with drugs, sex, and ungodly living. Some have even ended up taking their own lives, even though in the public's eyes, they have everything one could only dream about. Maybe you've found yourself trying to fill the vacuum in your life with career, fame, love, sports, money, relationship, power or sex. Unfortunately, unless the vacuum in your heart is filled by God, all these achievements will not make you feel happy or fulfilled.

2. To know God's master blueprint for your life

One of the most important reasons why you need to hear God's voice is because He created you. He has the master blueprint for your life, and He possesses the manual on how you can excel in this world. Before He created you, He had already planned the good works that He wants you to do (Ephesians 2:10). You can never truly know your destiny until and unless you hear His voice. If you fail to ask Him for the master blueprint for your life, you will be living on this earth without ever knowing the purpose for which He put you here. Many of us think that God's purpose is just to save us, give us eternal life, and then bring us to heaven when our time is up. Many of us live as though our passport is stamped "Heaven" as our final destination. Therefore, we just sit back, relax, and wait for the day when we will finally meet Him in heaven. If this were the only reason you were born, then God would have taken you to heaven once you were saved. Why are you still on this earth? The reason is that He wants you to complete the good works that He prepared for you to do. You will not know the good works that He has prepared for you if you don't ask Him or if you don't know how to discern His voice. He is the one who puts the passion, desires, and character in you. You are not just an accident of your parents. God in His love for you knew exactly when and where you would be born and who you would become. Even as you read this book now, He knows what you are facing and where you are living at this moment in time.

3. To know God as your GPS/compass in your life

If you do not learn to hear His voice, you will travel this journey of life without God's GPS/compass and you will live a directionless and purposeless life. His compass tells you what you should do next and what not to do. If you don't learn how to hear His voice, you will be like a mouse inside a maze that encounters blockage after blockage and is unable to proceed further. When you learn to hear His voice, He will direct your path so that you will have a life full of purpose, and you will be able to fulfill your destiny.

4. To know His great plans for your life

He is your heavenly Father and you are His child. He has great plans for your life and unless you communicate with Him, you will have no idea how to fulfill your purpose. If you don't speak to Him, you act as though you're not on talking terms with Him. You cannot have a relationship with your heavenly Father if you do not speak to Him and ask Him questions about your life. You also cannot have a relationship with Him if you don't tell Him about what you're going through and ask what you should do when you're at a crossroads. You shouldn't only talk to Him when you are in trouble. You should be developing an intimate relationship with Him even when everything is going fine. Then, when you are at a crossroads, you will already know His character and how He feels about you. You can, therefore, be confident that He cares about you and that He will direct you when you are facing a major decision. In fact, it is written in the Bible: *"And your ears will hear a word behind you, 'This is the way, walk in it, whenever you turn to the right or to the left"* (Isaiah 30:21).

Intimacy in any relationship takes time to develop and grow. Your heavenly Father desires to speak and longs to communicate with you. You only need to ask Him to teach and show you how to clearly recognize His voice and He will be happy to do so!

In Jack Deere's book, *Surprised by the Voice of God*, he made this observation:

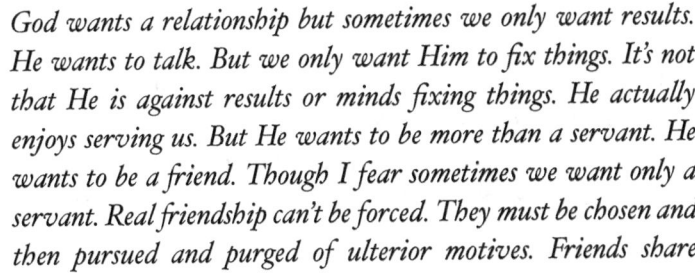

God wants a relationship but sometimes we only want results. He wants to talk. But we only want Him to fix things. It's not that He is against results or minds fixing things. He actually enjoys serving us. But He wants to be more than a servant. He wants to be a friend. Though I fear sometimes we want only a servant. Real friendship can't be forced. They must be chosen and then pursued and purged of ulterior motives. Friends share

secrets and understanding of each other grows—so does trust and appreciation. If the friendship deepens, one day you wake up and realize that you love your friend for who they are, not for what they can do for you. In fact, they don't need to do anything for you. Just being with your friend is the highest joy. Yet the truth is that there is nothing you wouldn't do for your friend and nothing your friend wouldn't do for you. Real friendship is love, and love must be given freely or else it is not considered as love (Song of Solomon 8:6-7). As long as we're primarily interested in our friend for what they can do for us, we'll never have a true friendship.

God has an overall plan and a future for you. However, you need to ask Him specifically about His plan and how you can fulfill it. One day, you will have to face Jesus at the Great White Throne and will have to give an account of what you have done with your life. Imagine how sad you will feel if you have achieved many things in your life, but none of them were what He had prepared for you to do. In the area of ministry, if you are honest with yourself, you may not always be serving with a pure motive. You may serve to be accepted, recognized, or because you are afraid to say "no." Frequently, you may go about "doing ministry" based on these wrong motivations and so actually never find fulfillment and excitement when you serve. When God shows you what He wants you to do, you will do it with a sense of excitement and purpose. You will not feel "compelled" to serve. You will not feel guilty or condemned when you have to say "no" to a request to serve when you know in your heart that, though it is a "good thing," it may not be a "God thing." Your first ministry is to love Him.

I was once asked to teach some Christian group leaders on how to hear God's voice. I encouraged these leaders to ask God to show them what He wanted them to focus on in their individual groups, even though each group had to follow the agenda set out by the church. However, since each group member is uniquely created, God longs to speak to them specifically and personally when they attend the Christian group each week.

None of the Christian leaders had ever asked God this important question before. After waiting upon the Lord, they shared what they'd heard from God regarding the direction of their individual group. It was exciting to hear that God had a different focus for each of the Christian groups. The focus of the different groups ranged from "building a foundation for strong marriages," to "reaching out to pre-believers by cooking," and "reaching out to non-believers through golfing." Four years later I spoke to the Christian group leader whose God-given focus was to "build a foundation for strong marriages." These leaders had since enrolled all their members on the 2=1 marriage program. These leaders had the joy of seeing all their members' marriages strengthened as a result of the training. If they had not asked God about the focus of the Christian group, they would have missed out on being used by God to help to build strong marriages in their members.

In her book, *Desperately Deeper*, Lana Vawser gave a fantastic reason for why we should learn to hear His voice. She wrote:

> *God is not looking for people who are going to do things for Him. He is looking for people who are desperate to hear His heart, grow in knowing His love, and follow His lead to do that which He calls them to do. If we cannot hear what the Spirit is saying, how do we know where the Spirit is leading? We are given the guidance in the Word of God, but the Lord also wants us living moment by moment hearing what the Spirit is saying. If we are not listening for what the Spirit is saying, then we guess what He wants us to do. We move forward on our own assumptions.*

Benjamin Schafer in his blog (*Practical Tips for Prophetic Ministry*) made this profound observation:

> *Many Christians seek God primarily for instruction. But God is much more interested in lovers than in workers. About 90% of what He tells us is about His heart and love for us. Only about 10% are instructions. That's because we are first His beloved*

and He is first a lover (Matthew 22:38; John 15:15). He wants to build friendships so much more than a workforce.

5. Hearing God's voice brings blessings

You are blessed when you hear and obey God's voice because you will be able to find your direction and the path to take. This will help you fulfill the purpose of your life (1 Corinthians 3:10-12; Romans 8:14). One of my friends shared that when his son was deciding which college degree to pursue, they sought God's direction. God showed them very clearly which college degree the son should enroll in, even though the son was keen to pursue another program. As they surrendered the decision to the Lord, they felt peace in their hearts. In hindsight, if the son had persisted in choosing the college degree he preferred, he would not have found a job after graduation. Four years later, the students who graduated from his preferred course could not find any jobs because the economy had changed. No one is able to know what will happen in four years' time with human logic alone. Your heavenly Father, who knows the beginning and the end, is able to guide you to the right decision. This is only possible if you allow Him into your life and obey His leading.

6. To prepare you for the things that are to come (John 16:13)

Many times you will encounter situations that are not pleasant. God in His mercy and love *prepares* you before the actual happening. One of my friends, Pat Y, told me that just before her position was made redundant, she had a vivid dream. In the dream, she was handed a check with a huge amount. She did not understand the meaning of the dream. However, when she was told about her job loss, she remembered the dream and it gave her much comfort. What was truly amazing was that when she was handed her redundancy check, it was the exact same amount as in her dream. The dream showed her about the future, and it has come to pass. Therefore, she had the confidence that God would provide another job for her. Indeed, in a short period, she was headhunted for a role she hadn't even applied for. Isn't God amazing?

When my son's position was made redundant, I was very concerned. One day while praying, the heavenly Father distinctly spoke to me regarding this situation. He said to me, "Why do you act as if what has happened to Ben is a surprise to Me?" I knew in my head that He knew this was going to happen to Ben. He is the one who wrote Ben's life before he was born. However, in my heart, I don't think I had the faith to believe it. My son and his wife had already booked a holiday before the job redundancy (severance package) occurred. This created some uncertainty as to whether they should cancel the trip in case a job opening should come up while they were away. However, a prophetic word was given to him that the new job would only come during the new year and that he and his wife were to go ahead and enjoy their holiday. What a loving Father we have, who knows our thoughts and concerns and lets us know ahead of time what will happen.

One of my friends, Pat L, went to the prayer mountain in Korea for a prayer retreat a few years ago. During that time, God distinctly told her that He would promote her. However, when she returned to Perth at midnight, the Holy Spirit prompted her to check her work email. When she read her work email, she was shocked to find that her position had been made redundant, and she had to apply for another higher position. She remembered what God told her in Korea and held on to that prophetic word, believing that she would be promoted. God's promise to her finally came to pass, and she was promoted. Praise the Lord!

7. To help you see yourself, others, and situations around you more clearly (Job 33:14-18)

Many times God speaks through dreams. The secrets of your heart and these revelations will help you see things more clearly. God always has a different perspective than you. If you fail to speak to Him, you may miss what He is doing in situations in your life that you may not even be aware of. When you receive a prophetic word for yourself or for others, suddenly there is clarity on the reason you are going through the situation. God will not only show you what you are facing currently but, in His love and mercy, He will also show you the outcome. That can bring much comfort to you, especially if all you can see is the darkness in front of you. You might wonder if you will ever come out of the dark tunnel. When God shows you coming out of the dark tunnel into the light through a prophetic word or dream, it will give you the hope and courage to go on.

When my husband Paul and I had to close a business we started, this resulted in a great financial loss to us. We were very discouraged. However, one day when we attended a church service, the pastor gave us a prophetic word that "our wilderness days are over." That prophetic word broke something in the spiritual realm for us. Our sense of hopelessness and discouragement dissipated, and we were able to look forward to coming out of that dark period in our lives.

8. To help you know His will and receive His guidance and direction in difficult situations (Psalm 16:7)

Your heavenly Father loves you very much. He reaches out to you, even when you don't seek Him concerning His will or guidance for your life. He can use dreams to counsel and instruct you (Job 33:14-18). He can even use what you watch on the television to guide and direct you. He is infinitely creative in getting your attention, even when you consciously or unconsciously do not or cannot hear His voice. One of my trainees mentioned that she loves to watch Korean movies and that God frequently uses Korean movies to speak to her concerning the situation she's facing.

There was a time when I was worried about a money situation because I couldn't find a tenant for my investment property. That night I had a dream that I was worshipping God at home. As I was worshipping, I saw something shining on the floor. I reached down and found that it was a blue sapphire diamond. I was overjoyed! I put it into my pocket and started walking to find my husband and son to show it to them. As I was walking, I felt something sharp in my pocket. When I reached inside my pocket, I took out a crisp, brand new $100 Australian dollar note. I put the note back in my pocket and happily and excitedly continued to look for my husband and son to show them the note. When I woke up, I asked God for the interpretation of the dream.

God told me that He was using the dream to remind me He is not limited by what I think about money nor the ways to earn money to meet my financial needs. Instead, He is able to provide money from anywhere, at any time, and in any form. He impressed upon my heart that money and gemstones can just appear in my life, for He is able to create something out of nothing. The dream gave me much comfort and confidence that He would provide whatever was needed for my family. Indeed, within a short period, He provided a tenant for me. What a faithful God we serve! I have also heard many testimonies from people whose debts have been supernaturally canceled because God has erased their debt records in the bank's database. I am trusting God to do the same for me!

Why you may not want to speak to God

You may have the wrong idea that God only speaks to "holy" or "spiritual" people. Since you may not think you are in this category, you might fear being rejected or reprimanded by Him. However, in case you think that God only wants to speak to holy people, remember that God searched out Adam and Eve after they sinned and disobeyed Him. He loved them so much that He even made garments of skin to cover them (He must be the first tailor!).

Just like some children who don't speak to their parents even though the parents long so much to speak with them, God is always longing to commune with you. Listed below are some reasons why you may not want to speak to God:

1. You think that God is angry with you

Many times, fear cripples you and takes away the desire for you to want or need to speak to God. You do not want to speak to God because you are afraid of being rejected or punished by Him due to sins in your life. You may feel that He will pour His wrath on you when you speak to Him, so you run away from Him and do not let Him into your life. If you say that you can't hear His voice or converse with Him, you are essentially implying that you are not on talking terms with your heavenly Father. You also don't want to talk to someone if you are angry with that person or if that person is angry with you. Many people think that God is an angry God because of what they read in the Old Testament due to the punishment that He metes out. God is a just God and so He has to punish wrongdoing. However, Jesus has already taken your punishment by dying on the cross for you. When God sees you, He sees you as righteous because of the finished work of Jesus on the cross. His anger has been turned away from you.

2. You think that God is not interested in speaking with you.

You may not be keen to speak to someone if you think they are not interested or keen to talk to you. Your parents may not show interest in hearing what is going on in your life. Though they are good parents, they may be consumed with earning a living and by the time they are home, they may not have the energy to talk to you. Such experiences with your earthly parents may make you think God has no time for you and that He has better things to do than to talk to you and listen to your concerns.

One of my mentors, Russell Walden from Father Heart's Ministry, gave this account. Once he was in a conference sharing what God had told him. Someone in the group stood up and retorted, "That is the problem that I have with people like you. You always say that God speaks to you. God has never spoken to me!" Russell then replied, "You mean to say that you are not on talking terms with your heavenly Father?" The truth is that we have accepted the abnormality of not hearing God's voice for such a long time that if someone says they can hear God's voice, we think it is abnormal. We've accepted the abnormal for so long that it has become normal to us.

Tony Dale in his book, *Being Still and Knowing* wrote:

> God has created a way of interacting spiritually with Him that far surpasses e-mail. Think of it this way: when we pray, we are sending Him our email, we pour out our deepest thoughts and feelings to Him, ask Him for forgiveness, guidance, and blessing. We bring our deepest concerns to Him and hit "send." But how many of us patiently wait for His reply? How is He supposed to

answer us if we don't check in for His reply? Communication is transmitting and receiving information. We are masters of transmission, but few have learned how to quietly wait and listen for His answers.

3. You think that you need to earn the right to speak to God.

When God created you, He put in you an antenna that can be tuned to the frequency of His voice. This means that you can hear Him. However, due to the busyness of your life or wrong teaching you have received, you may think hearing God's voice is for the elite few or for those who have achieved some sort of spirituality. If you think that you can never attain these perceived conditions or standards, you will not even bother to try. You may tell yourself, "Better not try to hear His voice so that I will not be disappointed." Many of us are in good company when we think this way. One of my trainees, Lee H, shared her feelings about her journey in learning to hear God's voice. She said:

> *I thought that I had to fulfill certain spiritual criteria such as being a leader in the church or reading the Bible every day before I could hear His voice. I always admired and envied people who could see visions or hear God speaking to them. I felt discouraged and wondered, 'Why I can't I be like them?'*

I am sure that you can relate to her struggle. I pray that as you read this book, you will begin to believe the truth that you do not need to "earn the right" to hear God's voice.

4. You fear that you may hear other voices and not His voice.

I believe that there is an innate desire in you to communicate with your heavenly Father. However, there is fear that you may end up hearing Satan's voice or your own voice when you try to hear God's voice. So instead of learning to recognize His voice, you may tend to take the safe option by shutting off this faculty of hearing, so you will not be deceived. I was so encouraged when J.J, a 9-year-old boy whom I taught, told me that he has learned that "there are three voices talking to me. The voices are my voice, God's voice, and the devil's voice. God's voice tells me to do the right thing. My own voice always starts with 'I.' The devil's voice tells me bad and negative things." Amazingly, this boy has defined so simply how to discern the various voices that he hears. In subsequent chapters, you will learn how to discern His voice from other voices.

Prayer

Dear heavenly Father, I do not always understand why You want to speak to me. I thought that You were only interested in people who are good, smart, or obedient. Sometimes I have the wrong thinking that You are too busy to want to speak to me. I thought that You are like my parents who do not always show interest in what is going on in my life or have the time to speak to me. Forgive me, heavenly Father, for having this wrong thinking about You. Help me to understand Your heart and how much You long to communicate with me. Teach me to hear Your voice as I continue to read this book. In Jesus' name. Amen.

Activation exercises

1. Dear heavenly Father, can You please show me/tell me/let me sense: "What do you want to speak to me regarding my relationship/self-image/career/studies/marriage?" (Write down what comes to your mind when you ask Him these questions.)

2. Dear heavenly Father, can You please show me/tell me/let me sense: "Why do You still love me when I have not really lived a life that is up to Your standard?" (Write down what comes to your mind when you ask Him these questions.)

SUMMARY

God desires to speak to you because He created you and loves you. He is not angry with you, but He is interested in every aspect of your life. You do not need to achieve a particular level of spirituality before He speaks to you. You need to hear God's voice because He has the master blueprint for your life. He wants to show you the direction that He wants you to take so you can fulfill the destiny that He has for you. When you hear His voice, He will direct and guide you in every decision that you make in your life so that you can fulfill His plans and purpose for your life.

God is not silent. It is the nature of God to speak.

—*A.W. Tozer*

2

WHO DOES GOD WANT TO SPEAK TO?

God speaks to every one of His creation, whether male or female, young or old, Christian or non-Christian. He can even speak to animals and nature too.

1. God speaks to both men and women

God speaks to both men and women. However, He may utilize different modes of communication because men and women use a different hemisphere of the brain to receive revelation from Him. Our brain is divided into the left and right hemispheres, the right hemisphere is the creative/intuitive side and the left is the logical side. Both sides exist for every person. Most males are more visual, and that is the reason the world finds it easy to hook them on pornography and computer games. Most females are more developed in their sensing, feeling, and hearing faculties as compared to most males. For example, none of the disciples could sense Jesus' anguish as He prepared Himself for the cross. However, Mary could sense His anguish and therefore she anointed him with oil. Jesus said it was for his burial (John 12:3-8). In 2 King 4:9 the Shunammite woman perceived, by the means of her senses, that Elisha was a holy man of God, even though no one else seems to have perceived this.

When the Holy Spirit speaks to you, He imparts into your spirit and you receive spontaneous thoughts, pictures, or words that suddenly pop into your thoughts. It seems that most men use more of the left (logical) side of their brain while most women use more of the right (creative/intuitive) side of their brain. This implies that if both a man and a woman receive the same thoughts or visions, the man will try to use the logical side of his brain. The man will tend to use his human reasoning to dismiss thoughts as being his imagination, own thoughts, or thinking. For people who use more of the logical side of the brain, they can learn to overcome relying on human reasoning by training their natural mind to enquire of the Holy Spirit. They can ask questions such as, "Holy Spirit, what do you want me to do about this?" or "Holy Spirit, how do I go about doing this?"

Les Crause in his book, *Perfecting Prophetic Ministry*, confirmed the difference between how men and women respond to revelation:

> *Most women are right-brained, and they tell us that the right brain is very intuitive. It is more open to allegorical thinking and revelation. Men are more left-brained and logical in their thinking, so they don't quickly respond to revelation. This means that men often take a while to get going in prophetic ministry because this ministry requires a lot of right-brained thinking. Women are far more open to the prophetic. And you will find that the Prophetic Movement probably has more women in it than men. This is because they are readier to open their hearts wide. They are ready to hear from the Lord, and to just jump into the river and swim.*

A few years ago, my husband wanted to buy a product from a salesman. Everything seemed to be in order and my husband was very keen to buy the product, but I had a nagging feeling that I couldn't trust this person, though I couldn't place the reason for this feeling. I think that I was using the right side of my brain to make the decision not to buy from this salesman. My sense/intuition proved right when the company he worked for discovered his involvement in fraudulent activities.

2. God speaks to children

Children hear God differently than adults because God brings His communication down to the level of the child. The mode in which He speaks to them may also be very different. He will speak to them using experiences and words they can understand. For example, it will be difficult for them to understand if God shows them a picture of something they do not know. God will, therefore, use something that is already in their vocabulary or experience to communicate with them. Children have a pure heart and they have no pre-conceived ideas. By their childlike faith, if we tell them they can hear God's voice, they will believe they can with all their hearts. They will not question as much as adults regarding all of the theology behind it.

Serene Huang, the Overseas Mission Director of Global Mission United, shared how her heart was stirred by God at a tender age for mission:

> *I was only eight when I picked up the Bible for the first time and read the unadulterated account of how Herod, in wanting to seek out Jesus, ordered that all infants be executed. I remember crying and placing the Bible on the floor. Going down on my knees, I interceded for all the children as far as the east is from the west, for God to please rescue, protect, and save every innocent child. With that first prayer, I stepped into what was to be my calling. At the age of 17, a prophet told me that I was to be a mother to many. And subsequently many similar prophesies were bestowed upon me. I received them all.*

Mark Virkler (Communion with God Ministry), in his article called "Training your Child to Encounter Jesus – Godly Imagination and Vision," wrote:

> *Once children are taught to use their imaginations, they step from godly imaginations (i.e. picturing things the Bible says are true), directly into visions, and they can do it a lot easier than adults.*

He shared a testimony of how Brent Engleman (www.ThePropheticTraining.com) trained his two-and-a-half-year-old son to use his imagination. Brent started the training by asking his son to picture in his imagination a simple picture such as a bus or other inanimate objects. Brent then trained his son to see living or animate objects such as a bird, elephant, dog and then to see his granddad. Subsequently, Brent trained him to see living things in motion. The next day, Brent's son shared that he had seen a vision of heaven and that he saw angels and Jesus.

It is so true what Mark Virkler said about how pure and childlike children are. I remember when I served in the children's church, I encouraged the children, aged 3 to 5, to quiet down after the worship session, and allow God to speak to them. Once during a session, I asked the children about what God was saying to them. One little boy said, "God said I must share my toys with my brother." Another girl said, "God said He loves me." Another girl said, "God asked me whether I love Him." Children are never too young to hear God's voice. Samuel heard God's voice when he was twelve years old.

In Cherie Fuller's book, *When Children Pray*, she wrote:

> *Children's ability to hear God is often unsullied by past experiences. They seem to have a way of knowing, of being tuned in to a divine wavelength. And if we listen to them, we can learn much occasionally something we really need to know.*

Bill Hybels shared his personal journey of hearing God's voice in his book, *The Power of a Whisper*:

> *Upon the occasion of hearing his second-grade teacher read the Old Testament story of Eli and Samuel and after class, Hybels relates he approached his teacher asking, 'Miss Van Soelen,' I said as my throat began to choke up, 'Does God still speak to little boys?' She smiled and let out a relieved sigh. Placing her two hands on my shoulders, she looked me square in the eye. 'Oh, yes, Billy,' she said. 'He most certainly does. And if you learn to*

quiet yourself and listen, He even will speak to you. I am sure of it.' I felt a swell of release as I considered for the first time in my seven years of life that perhaps Christianity was more than ancient rules, creeds and other stiff-necked ways. Maybe God really did speak. And maybe He'd speak to me.

Children can have an imagination as vivid as an adult. For example, if you ask them to imagine their favorite breakfast, they may even "taste" the orange juice and bacon in their imagination. Through their imagination, they can "revisit" the last holiday destination they most enjoyed.

Sometimes when a child has been through a difficult experience, they may smell things related to this experience. For example, if their house was previously burned down, they may smell smoke when they are anxious. Whenever they smell smoke, it may bring them back to the time when their house burned down and cause them to relive the traumatic experience again. A certain smell (whether pleasant or unpleasant) may also evoke a certain feeling or bring them back to that experience.

3. God speaks to animals and nature

In the Bible, the donkey Balaam was riding heard God's voice, saw an angel, and spoke (Numbers 22:3-30). God caused the frogs (Exodus 8:3-14), the insects (Exodus 8:16-17), and the locusts (Exodus 10:4-19) to go into Egypt. God caused hail and thunder (Exodus 9:18-26) to cover Egypt. God can speak to the sea (Exodus 14:15-16, 21) and cause the water to stop flowing and to start flowing again (Exodus 14:26). God can tell the snow to fall on the earth (Job 37:6) and for the rain to come as a mighty downpour (Job 37:6). In Jeremiah 10:13, God's voice caused the clouds to ascend from the end of the earth. He sends lightning with the rain and He brings out the wind from His storehouses. In Ezekiel 13:13, God caused a violent wind to break out. God can speak to the trees and they bear fruit. Psalm 29:3-9 records the animals and nature that God speaks to and the power of creation when He speaks:

> *The voice of the Lord is over the waters; the God of glory*

thunders, the Lord thunders over the mighty waters. The voice of the Lord is powerful; the voice of the Lord is majestic. The voice of the Lord breaks the cedars; the Lord breaks in pieces the cedars of Lebanon. He makes Lebanon skip like a calf, Sirion like a young wild ox. The voice of the Lord strikes with flashes of lightning. The voice of the Lord shakes the desert; the Lord shakes the Desert of Kadesh. The voice of the Lord twists the oaks and strips the forest bare.

In Genesis 7:6-9, Noah and his family went into the ark first. When the animals went into the ark, it was not because Noah went on a great roundup and drove them into the ark. God spoke to the animals, and they responded and went into the ark. God is the original Tarzan! He can speak to the animal kingdom better than Doctor Dolittle. God's voice, therefore, can communicate with all of His creation because He created them with the ability to hear and respond to His voice. He can command the locusts to devour the land (2 Chronicles 7:13). If God can communicate with insects and they respond to Him, how much more will He communicate with us whom He created in His image?

We find another example of God communicating with animals in the prophet Elijah's experience. When Elijah fled from Ahab, King of Israel, he went to an area east of the Jordan River. When he was there, God commanded ravens to bring him food (1 Kings 17:4-6). In Jonah 2:10, God commanded a fish to vomit Jonah onto dry land.

In 2004, when the tsunami occurred in Thailand, there were many humans who perished but surprisingly, there were no wild animals killed. It appears the animals knew that the tsunami was approaching and moved to higher ground and therefore, were not hurt. This is an example of God speaking to animals in the 21st century.

4. God can speak to people who do not know Him.

There are many accounts in the Bible of God speaking to people who don't know Him. In Matthew 27:19, Pilate's wife dreamed that Jesus was a righteous man. God used Jonah to speak to the people of

Nineveh (a pagan city) about the coming destruction of the city because of their wickedness. However, when they heard the word of God through Jonah, they believed God and all of them, including the animals, fasted and the people repented. These people were non-Jehovah believers, yet they heard and believed God through Jonah (Jonah 1-3).

Today, God is still speaking to non-Christians because of His great love for them and because He wants to bring them into His kingdom. In the article by Darren Carlson in TGC (The Gospel Coalition, US edition), "When Muslims Dreams of Jesus" (May 31, 2018), he wrote:

> *In 2007, Dudley Woodberry and others published a study that recounted interviews with 750 former Muslims who had converted to evangelical Christianity. Many of the reasons they gave for their conversion would be expected—the love of God, a changing view of the Bible, and an attraction to Christians who loved others. But one reason might come as a surprise: the experience of a dream they believed to be from God. These study results aren't isolated. Mission Frontiers magazine has reported that out of 600 Muslim converts, 25% experienced a dream that led to their conversion. The great missionary Lillias Trotter also reported dreams that drove Muslims to Christ.*

Recently I met a dear woman of God, Colleen M, and she shared that even though she grew up in a godly family, she never embraced the Christian faith and was into horoscope reading. She read her horoscope each day and believed everything that she read. One day, she read in the horoscope that she would meet a lady wearing a yellow dress and meeting this person would change her life. She believed what she read so much that she took her two children in her car and drove around to search for the lady who was wearing a yellow dress. She drove around for quite some time and was about to give up when she suddenly chanced upon a lady in a yellow dress, who was watering the plants in her garden. She stopped the car and approached her. The lady did not act surprised to see her and, after a brief conversation, the lady asked her whether she had a personal relationship with Jesus. This lady was able to lead her to know Jesus as her personal Savior. Who could imagine that God would use Colleen's involvement in the horoscope to lead her to Him? Only God can do this!

Recently, Pastor Peter Hammer from Centrepoint Church shared with me how God spoke to him when he asked for a sign to show that He is real:

> *I grew up in a great family but not a religious one. As a teenager, I was extremely quiet, reserved and insecure. I was finding my identity and our family was learning to manage with a diagnosis of mental illness in my mother. I remember clearly as a 14-year-old asking myself the question, 'What is the point to life?' It wasn't from a place of deep depression but rather searching for meaning and purpose. It was around this time that my neighbors, who'd emigrated from Singapore, invited me to go to church. For nine months I resisted the invitation, thinking that church was not a place for me. But God was working in my life and my need for the purpose in life was intensifying. Finally, after wrestling with the reality of God, I accepted an invitation to go to church on the first Sunday of 2000. The experience was positive though I didn't understand the salvation call. It was later that evening that my neighbors invited me to their home for dinner and I was asked if I would like to make Jesus my Lord and Savior. Though I had my doubts, I prayed from my heart that life-changing prayer. It was later that night though that I discovered just how real this God is. As I was going to bed later that night, I prayed, 'If you're real, would you show me a sign?' At 1 a.m. the next morning, the sign came. A fire had broken out in the park behind our house and emergency services had us on standby to evacuate. As curiosity took over, I went to see this fire and the moment I saw the flames, I experienced the presence of the Holy Spirit. At the time I couldn't have put words to the experience and even today the words don't do any justice but enough to say that it felt like waves of His love, His power, His grace was breaking over me. I heard that small but profound voice speaking into my spirit and soul validating my*

identity in Jesus and the purpose God would have for my life. It was literally and figuratively my burning bush moment.

Pastor Aaron Pryce from Centrepoint Church, Perth, shared the following testimony of how God spoke to him when he was in prison, an unbeliever, and how God gave him his life assignment.

> *I grew up in a normal home. My life had no direction and I was in a total pit with my identity crushed and made some bad choices. By the time I was 15 years old, I was using heroin daily. I was in a place of darkness. I ended up five and a half years in prison due to stealing and armed robbery to satisfy my drug habit. When I was in my teens, I met Keith who worked as a chaplain at the rehabilitation center which I attended previously. When I was in prison, he would come and visit me once a month. He would leave a letter for me to read with a Bible verse at the end of the letter. In 2004, on Good Friday, the prison had a special event and special visits were allowed for loved ones to visit the prisoner. Everyone has visitors except for me as I had burned all my bridges and, at 25 years old, I had no direction, no identity and I had alienated everyone who had loved me, except for my mum. That night, I read the letter that Keith had left me and the Bible verse at the end of the letter was Romans 8:39, 'For I am convinced that neither death nor life, neither angels nor demons, neither the present nor the future, nor any powers, neither height nor depth, nor anything else in all creation, will be able to separate us from the love of God that is in Christ Jesus our Lord.' Boom! It suddenly hit me like an explosion. It suddenly made sense to me that even though I had done so many things wrong, even though I was sitting in a prison cell, the love that He has for me cannot be taken away. He loves me even when I do not love myself. It was as if He was talking to me there and then. I remember saying that I did not want to live. I did not expect to live past 30 years old anyway. At that moment, I realized someone loves me and I questioned how He could love me when I didn't even love myself, nor did I*

even want to be alive. I heard Him speak back to me. He said, 'You may not want your life, but I want your life and I want all of your life.' At that very moment, I looked up and on my TV was the crucifixion scene from the movie, The Passion of the Christ. *God was trying to show me exactly what it was that His Son went through to give me redemption and to draw me into a relationship with Him. That changed my life radically. From that time onwards, everything changed. I had been taking drugs in jail. It stopped. Everything in my life changed. A year later, I was released from prison and I just knew that everything was different. I had the real sense that now that He had saved my life, I had to dedicate my life to Him. I remember asking Him, 'What do I do? How should I live? How do I pay You back?' God just said to me, 'Tell all people about the gift you have received.' That is what I have done ever since, telling people about the gift which I have received.*

A few months ago, I met Evangelist Kiran Murali (Jesus is Alive Ministries, Chennai, India). He shared how even before he knew God, he heard God's audible voice when he called out to Him in desperation:

> *I came from an orthodox Hindu family where our family owned many Hindu temples. For generations, we did our best to appoint priests to promote the unknown gods. But there was a day when my mother was attracted to the love of Jesus Christ through a true man of God. This sense of God's love brought my mother and my grandmother to become deeply rooted in Jesus Christ. All our family members were saved and worshiped Him, except me. I was a wild young person who wanted to explore all the temptations of the world and I was totally not interested in God. Many preachers used to visit our home to pray and bless our family. They used threats to threaten me that my fate will be to end up in hell if I would not accept Christ as my Lord. As a young person, I just wanted to enjoy the pleasures of the world and I was not the least concerned about where I was going to*

end up when my life on earth ended. As my life was rooted in the temptation of sin, I found myself in a state where sin had overpowered my life. I was devastated, hopeless, frustrated and I felt like a failure who was rejected by everybody. Nobody believed in me and I was a spectacle amongst all my relatives. I sincerely tried to find a way out with all my strength, but I failed.

One day, thoughts of suicide were engulfing my conscious mind. It was telling me that I couldn't succeed, and I couldn't come out of this situation and that nobody believed in me. This thought was battling in my mind. I was a bit drunk and was smoking at a junction surrounded by at least fifty other people. I broke down and started to cry. In my deepest anguish, I shouted saying, 'Jesus, if you are God, I don't need you. I want a friend, a true friend.' I cried out of my despair and fury. It was in this deepest depression and battle that something happened to me. I encountered our blessed Lord's compassion. Glory be to God! I heard him say, 'My son, fear not, I am with you.' Those audible words that I heard in my heart changed my life. I was shocked to know that God actually spoke to me when I was living in such a sinful life. He never pointed out my mistakes or my failures, He simply spoke to me. I was amazed that when I was in such desperation and in need of a true friend, He spoke to me while I was still in sin.

What a great testimony by Evangelist Kiran and what great love is shown by our heavenly Father who reached out to him when no else could. The world has worshiped numerous gods that can't even be counted, but no god can claim what Jesus says, "*I no longer call you servants, because a servant does not know his master's business. Instead, I have called you friends, for everything that I learned from my Father I have made known to you*" (John 15:15). In Romans 5:8, we read, "*But God demonstrates His own love for us in this: While we were still sinners, Christ died for us.*"

Many of us may not have such a dramatic testimony to share like Evangelist Kiran, Pastor Aaron, Pastor Peter or Colleen, but all of us have heard God's voice before we even knew Him. The reason is that God is the one who is making the first move towards us. In Isaiah 65:1, God declares, "*I revealed myself to those who did not ask for me; I was found by those who did not seek me. To a nation that did not call on my name, I said, 'Here am I, here am I.'*" No wonder all of us can testify how one day we heard the Good News that Jesus died for our sins and that our sins are forgiven, and our hearts were stirred. We felt the prompting to respond to the invitation to ask Jesus to come into our hearts. This may have happened while we were at a church service, or while we were still in the dumps. It could even be during a near-death experience. I have heard many testimonies of people who heard the Good News and invited Jesus into their hearts just before they took their last breath. They are in heaven now, cheering on their loved ones to run and finish the race of life with joy.

Who are you that you can speak to God?

Many of you might feel that you must attain a certain level of spirituality before God will want to speak to you. However, this is never a prerequisite of your heavenly Father. He wants to speak to you at all times, regardless of where you are in life. The strategy of the enemy is to encourage people to operate in a religious spirit. These people will demand that you need to attain some level of spirituality to earn the right to communicate with the Almighty God. Your heavenly Father communicates with all His creations. He will definitely communicate with you as you are made in His own image and have His DNA. He knows you by name. If God can use a donkey to communicate with a person, how much more will He communicate with you because you are His child? It is not about *you* but about a loving Father who longs to communicate with you. In fact, He says that if you want to enter/see the kingdom of God, then you must be like a little child (Matthew 18:3). People who operate in the realm of the legalistic and religious spirits will put many demands and man-made regulations on you. However, nowhere in the Bible does it say that "only mature, spiritual, and obedient sheep hear My voice." The words in John 10:27 clearly state that *"My sheep hear My voice."* That means that there is no exemption, exclusion or exception.

You may think God only speaks to His favorite children. You may never fathom why God, who is in heaven, would want to speak to an earthling like you, especially when you are just an ordinary person. However, in God's eyes, you are unique. You are one-of-a-kind and there is no one else like you. You need to remember that God loved Hagar, a slave/servant girl to Abraham, so much, that when she was running away, pregnant and scared, He spoke personally to her (Genesis 16:7-9). In our culture, we don't have much honor or respect for servants. From this account in the Bible, I am so thankful that God is no respecter of people and we are all precious to Him.

God loves you so much that He is interested in every intimate detail of your life. Even though He is in heaven, He is near to those who are contrite in spirit (Psalm 34:18). He is the one who created you. God has the blueprint of your life in His mind and He will let it be fulfilled in your life.

You need not behave like a mouse that is trapped in the maze. You might think that God is looking at you from the top of the maze as you move round and round in circles in your attempt to get out. You might feel angry that He sees what you are doing but doesn't seem to care enough to reach out to you. Even though it may seem no one cares about you or cares enough to talk to you (many people feel ignored and have low self-worth and low self-esteem), you need to know that when God sees you, He sees you through Christ and what He did for you on the cross. You are justified and qualified to be reconciled with God because of the great price Christ paid to bring you back to a rightful relationship with your heavenly Father.

Below are some reasons that you might believe that you are not qualified to speak to God:

1. You feel you are not spiritual enough.
2. You don't attend church regularly.
3. You smoke, drink, or use drugs, swear and use bad/foul

language.
4. You are not smart, pretty, or articulate like your friends or your siblings.
5. No one really notices you, so why would God notice you and want to speak to you?
6. You are too old.
7. You feel disappointed and grumpy that even your own children don't have the patience to listen to you.
8. You became a Christian recently and are too young in the faith.
9. You have not yet been baptized in the Holy Spirit.
10. You don't read the Bible regularly and have only a basic understanding of the Bible.
11. You don't know how to pray, nor do you pray regularly.
12. You are shy and don't feel confident to have a conversation with anyone, much less with God.
13. You are practicing an alternative lifestyle (homosexuality) and you are sure that would disqualify you.

The above list is not exhaustive, and I am sure that some readers may have more reasons to add to this list. The good news is: **Jesus Christ has justified and qualified you to hear God's voice.**

You may have been told the lie that you have to be good enough before a holy God will allow you to speak to Him. You may fear punishment from Him because you know that your life does not meet up to His holy standard. There are also many wrong teachings that tell you that you are not worthy of approaching God to speak to Him. You may have been told that you need to go through another holy person (for example, the priest or pastor) so that this person can speak to God on your behalf.

You are correct that by your own strength, ability, and character, you can never achieve the standard required to approach a holy God. However, because Jesus finished the work on the cross, you are justified and made righteous. Therefore, when you stand before God, He sees you righteous through Christ. So, whatever station of life you are at, or no matter what names the world calls you, our Creator, the heavenly Father, wants to speak to you. Take the step of faith. Do the activation exercises below; you will be surprised that God has always been speaking to you. In God's eyes, you are His child, whom He lovingly created. He loves you very much. He just loves to speak to you, and you don't have to earn the right to speak to Him.

A Filipino lady who was then a very young Christian attended one of my training sessions. As it was near the December holiday season, she was planning to go to the Philippines to visit her family during the Christmas break. She mentioned that she had a brother who was a Catholic residing there. I encouraged her to use the notes I had handed out to teach her brother to hear God's voice. When she returned to Perth, she told me that her brother was not only able to hear God's voice but he also "saw" visions. She was so surprised that a Catholic could hear God's voice—and also chuffed that she, a beginner herself, could be used by God to activate her brother to hear His voice. A wonderful testimony of God working in us and through us and this is truly encouraging!

A woman who had missed my training session came in just as I was handing out the notes at the end of the session. She was preparing to go on a mission trip to Cambodia the very next day, so she picked up a copy of my notes and left. In Cambodia, she was able to use the notes to activate the people in the church and was surprised they could hear His voice soon after the activation.

One of the young girls I taught shared that she saw angels standing next to the evangelist who was ministering at a healing crusade. This happened only a few months after she learned how to hear God's voice at one of my training sessions. She also shared that she saw vividly the angels throwing balls of fire at the people who had come up to the front to receive prayer for healing during this healing crusade.

These testimonies clearly show that all of us can hear His voice. He is the one who makes the first move towards you. It's in His nature to communicate with you so that He can show you how much He loves and cares for you.

Prayer

Dear heavenly Father, sometimes I feel that I don't deserve to have You speak to me. I think I am too sinful to speak to You. I'm also an introvert and have difficulties connecting with people, so I believe I would experience difficulty in connecting with You too. I now realize this is the lie of the enemy. You care enough about me to want to connect with me and I really want to connect with You and hear Your voice. I want to personally experience You speaking to me. I know that when I hear Your voice, it will be an experience that the enemy cannot take away from me. Open my eyes so I can see You and open my ears, so I can hear You. Please remove any anxiety, doubt, fear, and unbelief so that nothing can hinder me from hearing your voice. In Jesus' name. Amen.

Activation exercise

Go to a quiet place to prepare yourself to hear His voice. Have a piece of paper so you can write down or draw what He shows you. You can write down the thoughts that come to your mind (spontaneous thoughts) as you ask Him the questions below:

1. Dear heavenly Father, can you please show me/tell me/let me sense: "What do you think of me?" (In Psalm 139:17-18, it says if I were to count the number of thoughts You have of me, it will be more than the sands of the sea.) The Holy Spirit may show you a picture in your mind. You may hear a Bible verse or a sentence, or you may hear a song. You may feel or sense His love and His smiling face beaming at you. Write down everything you see/hear/sense.

2. Dear heavenly Father, can you please show me/tell me/let me sense: "What is one of Satan's lies that I have believed which made me feel worthless or condemned? Please show me the truth about me." Write down what He has shown you.

SUMMARY

God longs to speak to every one of us regardless of whether we are young, old, male or female. If He speaks to animals and insects and non-Christians, He will surely speak to you since you have been created in His own image. Do not believe the lies of the enemy that tell you that you need to be "qualified" or "good enough" before God can speak to you. You have been justified and qualified in Christ. He has clothed you with His righteousness. You can, therefore, embark on this adventure of personally hearing Him speak to you.

Some people can be so disoriented to God that when He begins to work around them, they actually become annoyed at the interruption!

—Henry T. Blackaby, *Hearing God's Voice*

3

WHEN DOES GOD SPEAK TO YOU?

Your heavenly Father is reaching out to you all the time. In Isaiah 65:1-2, He says, *"I revealed Myself to those who did not ask for me; I was found by those who did not seek me. To a nation that did not call on my name, I said, 'Here am I, here am I.' All day long I have held out my hands to an obstinate people, who walk in ways not good, pursuing their own imaginations."*

God is speaking all the time. He can speak to you when you are admiring nature or when you are reading the Bible or meditating. He speaks when you ask Him questions. He speaks to you when you feel lonely, sad, happy, fearful, or discouraged. He is in every situation you face. He is never far away for He has already promised that He will never leave you nor forsake you (Hebrews 13:5). God has no problem communicating with you, the problem lies with you not being able to tune in to hear and listen to His voice. His voice is always transmitting, but the receiver (that is you) may not always be receiving what is being transmitted by Him. Blackaby wrote in the book, *Experiencing God*, "*If a Christian does not know when God is speaking, he is in trouble at the heart of his Christian life.*"

He has spoken since creation, from the times of the Old Testament to the New Testament. Unfortunately, sometimes when God speaks to you, it's not at a convenient time for you. You want to give Him a certain timeframe in which to answer you. If He does not respond to you in your timeframe, you walk away from the conversation. Many times, at the least expected place and time, He will suddenly drop a thought into your heart and give you the answer you have been waiting for. Frequently, it's when you are not thinking about anything in particular that God may suddenly speak to you. This could be at the least likely place, e.g. while you are using the toilet or taking a bath or brushing your teeth.

Jack Deere in his book, *Surprised by the Voice of God* wrote:

> *If we want a deep friendship with God, it is important to cultivate a state of mind where we view all our time as God's time, a state of mind where we are totally available to Him. It is necessary to do this because God speaks to us at the most inconvenient times. Sometimes He even lets His favorite servants spend time, energy and money in organizing a missionary journey. Then He waits until they get in the middle of that journey and forbids them to engage in ministry. Paul and his friends made plans to minister in Asia, but God wanted them in Europe (Acts 16:6-10). He lets them 'waste' time, money and energy before He redirects them there. It seems God almost delights in speaking to us at the most inconvenient times in order to test our availability. God gives us opportunities to demonstrate our real desire for Him by our attentiveness to His voice when it comes to us at the most inconvenient times or in the feeling and vague ways of dreams or impressions.*

1. God speaks every time you read His Word.

God speaks in many different ways, mainly and powerfully through His Word. God's word is living and active (Hebrews 4:12). When you read the Bible, you must not read it like stories that have happened to various people, but you must read it as a source of life-giving revelation. When you open the Bible, His voice is available to you in every moment, situation, and predicament you face. Through His Word, He reveals His will to you because He has given you the Holy Spirit to guide you into all truth (John 16:13). The Bible tells us that we should not live by bread alone but by every word (Rhema) that comes out of the mouth of God (Deuteronomy 8:3). The Holy Spirit breathes every word spoken and is full of the Spirit and life (John 6:63) and His word can change the situation you are facing. Unfortunately, for many of us, reading His Word is routine and a discipline we follow to satisfy our need to get it done and tick the box. You experience guilt and condemnation when you don't read His Word, so you rush through it to appease your conscience. You can glean so many truths and gems when you read the Bible. When God speaks through His Word, He invites you to come and seek Him. The truth is that the Word of God must transform you into His image as His Word washes over you (2 Timothy 3:16).

2. God can speak anytime during the day or night.

When God called Samuel by his name, it was at night while he was trying to sleep (1 Samuel 3:4-11). In 1 Samuel 3: 10, Samuel replied, *"Speak, for your servant is listening."* God speaks to you when you are listening; when you are attentive and ready to do whatever He asks.

I remember a season in which God woke me up exactly at 3 a.m. each morning. It was as if the alarm clock rang suddenly and I was fully awakened. I sensed that God was the one who woke me up because there was something He wanted to say to me, or He wanted me to intercede for someone. In obedience, I prayed in the Spirit. Whoever He put in my thoughts, I asked the Holy Spirit to help me pray the perfect prayer for that person. Sometimes, God doesn't show me who I'm to pray for, so I will just pray in the Spirit. One night when God woke me up, the Spirit of intercession was so strong that I had to go to another room to pray so as not to disturb my husband's sleep. After an extended period of prayer, God lifted the burden and I felt peace. Though I never knew who or what I was praying, I sensed that God was using me to intercede for someone who was in great danger on that day.

When does God respond to you after you have spoken to Him?

1. God can respond to you at any time.

God can respond to you at any time and anywhere. Normally when you prepare your heart and find a quiet place to hear His reply to you, you somehow know that it is Him speaking. Sometimes, you may rationalize why He may not want to answer you. You may also make the mistake of wanting Him to fit into your human time frame. Frequently, you do not wait for Him to reply because you want an instant answer from Him (like when you warm up something in the microwave and set the timer; you expect God to answer you when the timer goes off!). To justify your actions, you tell everyone, "I asked God, but He did not answer me. I can't wait any longer, so I will do what I have initially planned to do." You need to understand that God's ways are not your ways and His thoughts are not your thoughts and His time frame is not your time frame. You can't force God's hand to give you an answer within your time frame. If God does not answer within your expected time frame, it does not mean that He doesn't love you. Neither does it mean that He doesn't care for you nor that He hasn't heard you when you speak to Him.

You may get agitated and upset when you don't hear from Him in your expected time frame. Sometimes He may be testing your faith, and you feel He isn't responding to you. When you get impatient, it is easy to take things into your own hands. It is like Saul who was impatient while waiting for Samuel in 1 Samuel 13:8-13. Samuel had told Saul, *"Go down ahead of me to Gilgal. I will surely come down to you to sacrifice burnt offerings and fellowship offerings, but you must WAIT seven days until I come to you and tell you what you are to do"* (1 Samuel 10:8). Saul was worried that his whole army would desert him, so he offered the sacrifices himself, just before Samuel arrived and this was in direct disobedience to God's word spoken to him through Samuel. His impatience cost him his kingdom

Recently, Susan Lam, one sister I taught, shared the following testimony about her husband:

> *When he was in his 30's, my husband, HC, received a prophetic word that he has the anointing of Caleb and that he will serve God in his old age. Fast forward twenty-five years, we left our previous church unexpectedly and moved five years ago to another church. It is a very comfortable church, and we thought we would 'retire' in this church and perhaps serve in the bare minimum capacity. In 2018, the pastor asked us to join a new church plant. Both I and my husband were so comfortable in our retirement state and it would be no joke to start all over again when we are already so old. But the prophetic words of the pastor who prayed over HC came to his mind. It reminded him of the anointing of Caleb. Caleb served God till his old age and Caleb at age eighty-five was still not ready to retire. Caleb waited forty years to conquer the land. For HC, it's been thirty years since that prophetic word was given to him. The prophetic word remained in him, and in obedience, at age sixty-one, he responded. We crossed over to this new church plant and thus fulfilled the prophetic word of God that was spoken thirty years ago to him.*

This testimony is powerful, as it shows that every word that God has spoken over your life will come to pass. However, it may not come according to your own timing. You must learn to be patient for God's spoken word (Rhema) to take time to be fulfilled. You must not take things into your own hands or make things happen in your own timing or in your own way. Abraham and Sarah made the mistake of using their human thinking and effort by trying to make God's word about having a child come to pass (Genesis 16:1-4).

2. God may respond through anyone or by any means.

Many times, when you least expect it, God answers. God can speak through someone or even speak when you are watching the television. Suddenly, what someone said on the television was the answer you were asking Him for. Many people have testified that when they were driving, suddenly a vehicle in front of them had the answer that they were looking for on the license plate. God speaks back to you in mysterious ways and at any time He sees fit.

3. Sometimes God does not speak at all.

There may be times in your life when it seems as if you do not hear a thing from God. Some people call this the "quiet season" or the "dark night of the soul" (also known as the wilderness or the times when the heavens are like brass). During these seasons, it seems as if God is concealing Himself from you. This concealment is to induce you to search for Him, so He may reveal Himself to you. The late John Paul Jackson in his training course, *The Art of Hearing God*, explained what is happening in such times:

> *God is removing our singular reliance on natural, external vision so we can improve in seeing things the Holy Spirit reveals. God promotes a new vision, insight, and revelation to create a higher realm of understanding and trust in us, so we will live by faith and not by sight. During the dark soul of the night, we have difficulty finding and entering God's presence to hear from Him. Everything we know to do and have done before doesn't work.*

When your faith is being tested by God, it is easy to doubt God's love for you. You realize the truth that your faith is fragile, though you may believe you have strong faith. In such times, your emotions will want to take over and give you many negative thoughts. When you are going through this sort of situation, you must attempt to silence your emotions and declare in faith that God has promised He will never leave you nor forsake you (Hebrews 13:5). You need to understand God is still with you, *even* if you feel nothing. Every fiber of your being may tell you that God does not care or love you. In such seasons, when you cannot discern what He is doing in your life, you need to reflect on His faithfulness which He has demonstrated to you in the past. As you reflect on how He has brought you through in the past, you will learn to have the faith to trust that He can do it again.

When you are going through difficult times, it is important to have like-minded Christian friends who are willing and able to stand alongside you and uplift you in prayers. During such dark seasons, you may also encounter "Job's comforters." These are comforters who make you feel guilty by implying that you must have sin in your life for God to forsake you. My advice to you is to get as far away as possible from such people, for they will drag you down with their wrong theology of God's character. The wrong theology is that God is there for you only if you have no sin in your life. You must remember that God pardons sin and forgives your transgression. He will tread your iniquities under His foot, and He will cast all your sins into the depths of the sea (Micah 7:18-19). When you are going through the wilderness experience, God's love and faithfulness for you will bring you much comfort. *He doesn't change* regardless of what you feel or think. You can rest as you put your trust in His love, which is your sure foundation. God will never disappoint you and you must always remember that God's silence does not equal His absence or inactivity. He is always working behind the scenes of your life for your ultimate good and to bring glory to His name.

What are the reasons when God seems silent?

1. God has already spoken but you have not been obedient to do what He has asked you to do.

There may be times when you feel that God is silent, and you hear absolutely nothing at all, even though you have positioned yourself to listen to Him. This may be scary and frustrating and sometimes in your attempt to strive to "hear" Him, you may take matters into your own hands. When you experience God's silence, you should check to see if there is anything that God has already spoken to you to which you have not responded or obeyed yet. Many times, He will not give you new directions if you have not done what He has already asked you to do.

God may also be silent when you have asked Him the same question before, and He has already answered you previously. In such a situation, you should go back to the last time God spoke to you. You should ask yourself if you were obedient to Him at your last point of contact and conversation with Him.

2. God is testing you.

If you experience difficulties in hearing Him, even though you have obeyed the last thing He has asked you to do, it's possible that you are in a period of testing. He does not speak when you are taking a test. Now reflect on the last time you took a test. When you were taking the test, even if you raised your hand and tried to ask a question, the exam proctor/invigilator wouldn't answer you. Similarly, there will come a time in your life when, for an extended period, God has already instructed you and showed you His character and His nature. He may want to see whether you can stand the test based on your knowledge of His character and nature that He has shown you previously. You may keep doubting His love for you, even though He has shown His faithfulness and love to you time and again. In such times, I think God is saying to you, "My child, grow up and mature in your faith. Do not remain a child throughout your faith journey!" God's silence forces you to grow in trusting Him. This could be when you are walking in darkness or when you lack a sense of direction. When you come out of the darkness, you will eventually realize that He was with you all along. When you are going through such situations, Isaiah has this encouragement for you: *"Who among you fears the Lord and obeys the word of his servant? Let him who walks in the dark, who has no light, trust in the name of the Lord and rely on his God"* (Isaiah 50:10).

During your prosperity, it is difficult to know whether you have a love for God or only for His blessings. It is when you are going through trials that your faith is being tested. In the Bible, God left Hezekiah alone to test him that He might know all that was in his heart (2 Chronicles 32:31). God dealt with his pride by withdrawing from him. In Exodus 20:20, Moses told the Israelites that God tests them, so they may not sin. In Judges 3:4, God left the enemies in Canaan to test whether the Israelites would obey His commandments.

3. God is whispering.

Sometimes, though God may appear to be silent, He is lowering His voice to a whisper and, in order for you to hear Him, you must move closer to Him. For example, if someone lowers his/her voice when he/she speaks, you need to move closer, so you can hear that person.

Once I was teaching a class. The students were particularly noisy. I tried to shout to quiet them down, but they could not hear me over their own noise. So, I suddenly stopped talking loudly and whispered. They realized that I was whispering, so they stopped talking loudly in order to hear me. In the same way, sometimes God stops speaking completely. He lowers His voice to a whisper, so you can move closer to Him. He does not want you to go through the motion of hearing His voice, but He wants you to develop the intimacy He so much desires to have with you.

Though God is constantly pursuing you, He also wants you to pursue Him. In a relationship, the interaction between both sides is important. When only one party puts in all the loving effort, and the other doesn't react with love towards that person, it can be quite tiresome— or worse, bonding becomes weak! Remember, God loves you and He wants you to show your love for Him by loving Him back!

4. God is affirming that you are on the right track.

God's silence is not because He is angry or has rejected you, but it could be His way of affirming that you are on the right track. This is because you have already learned how to make godly decisions based on what you have learned from Him. God loves it when you ask Him questions. He also desires for you to mature into someone who will learn to allow His wisdom to guide you in making wise decisions. I have heard of people claiming that they asked God about everything, including what they should wear and eat each day. Just imagine how you would feel if your 30-years-old son asked you each day what he should wear and eat. You would be very sad and disappointed if your son has not even learned how to make such simple day-to-day decisions at that age.

5. God is not silent, but He has changed His channel of communication with you.

Sometimes you may think God is silent when in fact He has just changed His channel of communication with you. He is still communicating with you, but He is now using a different wavelength. He does this when you are so used to a certain way of receiving the communication from Him and you are starting to "take Him for granted." This can happen when you become prideful and boast that you have become an "expert" in hearing Him. You may be so used to Him speaking to you through the visual mode that you may "miss" it when He speaks to you through the auditory mode. This is true for those who may think a particular way of communication is "superior and more spiritual" than others.

Bill Johnson, in his book, *Dreaming with God*, explained it in this way:

> *Occasionally, we go through times when we feel God is not speaking to us. Whilst that may be so, most of the time He has simply changed His language, and He expects us to adjust with Him.*

In his book, *The Beginner's Guide to Hearing God*, Jim Goll gave the following insight about God being silent:

> *It's not that God has quit speaking. It's that He has just switched channels on His dial. It's like God uses a radio when He speaks to us. God has not quit speaking to you. He has just turned the knob over to a different channel that you are not used to hearing Him on. Our Father's voice comes to us in such a great variety of ways that we need such moments of enlightenment. Otherwise, we tend to get locked into set patterns. It's so good of God to temporarily shut down one channel in order to open up another. He hasn't quit speaking; He is opening our hearts and minds to hear His voice in new ways. He does this so that we will continue to grow progressively in our relationship with Him. He doesn't want us to become locked into the same patterns of hearing Him. God's goal is to have a real, live relationship with us. To tell the truth, He likes messing with our radio dial! Sometimes He turns the volume louder and then backs down,*

thus creating a greater dependency on Him. He loves to roll the dial to different stations to help us learn to appreciate the diversity within the Body of Christ. After we have logged a few more listening hours, we are a whole lot less frustrated with who controls the knobs. Eventually, we learn to love the wide variety of ways in which He speaks.

Mike Bickle in his book, *Growing in the Prophetic*, gives this advice to those who are encountering God's silence:

> God is silent, not due to one's rebellion but because He is setting up the situation that will bring more blessing to the person at a later time. In this case, some sincere though immature believers are confused by thinking that the silence of God is a sure sign of His displeasure and abandonment. Because some people experience long periods of silence from heaven, they wrongly conclude that God has withdrawn from them or that they have sinned grievously in some way. They fall prey to accusation, condemnation, and rejection.

When can you speak to Him?

1. No specific or any particular time is required

There is no specific or particular time that you can speak to God, just as long as you do speak to Him. Some people find that speaking to Him early in the morning works best for them while others prefer lunchtime or night time.

I used to think our heavenly Father would only speak to me when it was late at night because I am a night person. However, He has spoken to me many times on my way to work and even when I'm in a noisy environment and surrounded by people. I have learned never to tell Him that only night time works well for me but instead to be open to Him speaking to me at any time. I want my communication channels with God to be open at all times. This means that I can communicate with Him early in the morning, in the afternoon, during lunchtime, in the evening, at night and even when I am sleeping. I must consciously not put God in a box and that means even if I'm not thinking of speaking to Him, He can speak to me instead. He is available for you to speak to Him 24/7, so you should also learn to let Him speak to you 24/7, even when you are asleep (Job 33:15-18). Do you know that when you are asleep, your spirit is awake? Time or space should not dictate to you when He can speak to you and when you can speak to Him if you want to develop this level of intimacy with Him.

2. When you are facing troubles or difficulties in your life

In the book of Psalms, you read about David expressing his emotions and feelings—whenever he felt troubled, he turned to God. The Bible also records the times when His people called out to God when they were in trouble and God heard and answered them. When you are feeling lost and not sure what to do, you can talk to Him. He is interested in every minute detail of your life, and He wants to hear from you all the time, not only when you are in trouble! You will certainly feel sad if your children only talk to you when they are in trouble or when they need something from you. Likewise, you can imagine how God feels when you come to Him only when you need Him to do something for you. God wants an intimate relationship with you—and it pleases Him when you come into His presence, regardless of the situation you're in.

3. When you present your requests and petitions to Him

God encourages you to come to Him about anything. No request, petition or prayer is too small or insignificant for Him to answer. He reminds you not to be anxious about anything, but in every situation, by prayer and petition, with thanksgiving to present your requests to Him (Philippians 4:6).

4. Whenever you have feelings, no matter what they are (e.g. happy, sad, angry or disappointed)

You can speak to God about what you are going through in your life. Many times, your earthly parents may not want you to speak to them when you are angry. They wait for you to calm down before they allow you to speak to them. Maybe your earthly parents didn't want to hear about how you felt, so you learned to shut down your feelings in their presence. Because of this conditioning, you may think that you will be at ease speaking to God only when you are feeling spiritually well and everything is fine in your life. This doesn't make sense—don't you think that you really need to speak to Him even more when you are going through a difficult situation?

I remember an incident of a friend's son, who was clearly upset over some issues and was crying. The father demanded that the son stop crying but no matter how hard he tried, he just couldn't stop the tears, which made my friend furious. I was worried that my friend's son would grow up thinking that men should be tough and crying is a bad thing for men. Sadly, many men think they should not speak to God when they are sad or when they are crying. But know this: As a mother comforts her child, so will God comfort you (Isaiah 66:13). God keeps track of all your sorrows, and He collects and records all your tears (Psalm 56:8). As God said to King Hezekiah, so He will say this to you, "*I have heard your prayer. I have seen your tears*" (2 Kings 20:5).

Do you know that even when you feel upset with God, He still cares and loves you? You can never fathom how much the heavenly Father loves you. Even though you run away from Him instead of talking to Him about your pain and upset feelings, He is always reaching out to you. You can, therefore, speak to Him regardless of how you feel. He is a heavenly Father who completely understands you. When you experience anger, hurt, or disappointment, you may tend to turn away from Him instead of towards Him. The prayer on the next page can help you verbalize to Him how you feel.

Prayer

Dear heavenly Father,

Most of the time, I call upon you when I am in trouble or when I am angrily clenching my fists at You. Even though You say I can speak to You at any time, my tendency is to run away from You when my feelings overwhelm me or when I am angry or disappointed with You. Please help me realize that You love me regardless of how I feel about You or about myself. Help me sense Your presence when You are reaching out to me and help me respond to Your love and comfort during those difficult times. I want to have an intimate relationship with You to the extent that I am comfortable in approaching You at any time and no matter how I am feeling. In Jesus' name. Amen.

Activation exercises

1. If you would pause here and pray: "Heavenly Father, I am stopping right now and positioning myself to hear from You. Heavenly Father, can you please let me feel Your thoughts towards me? Let me sense Your love and presence in a tangible way. Let me hear You say that You love me. Let me see a picture of You hugging me and feeling Your loving arms around me." Now quiet yourself and let this be an intimate time between you and Your heavenly Father. Let Him know what you are feeling and speak to Him regarding what is on your mind.

2. In Revelation 3:20, Jesus says, *"Here I am! I stand at the door and knock. If anyone hears my voice and opens the door, I will come in and eat with that person, and they with me."* Visualize in your imagination, Jesus standing at the door of your heart and knocking at it. What is your response to His request for you to open the door? Write down what you will say or ask Him when you open the door to Him.

3. "Heavenly Father, I have a question I want to ask you. I will wait patiently for an answer from you: Heavenly Father, can you please show me/tell me or let me sense by smell, touch or taste: "What is one aspect of Your character that You want to reveal to me so I can know you better?" Quiet your heart and spirit and write down what you sense/see/hear. Write down what He says to you. If you don't get an

answer immediately, just go about your normal activity and if a sudden thought or picture comes to your mind, write it down.

SUMMARY

God can speak to you at any time, anywhere. Sometimes He may appear to be silent for some reason or purpose; He is not angry or ignoring you. Though you may have the tendency to speak to Him only when you are in trouble, He wants you to know that He is available 24/7 and is there for you when you feel you need someone to talk to or simply need a friend. It thrills His heart when you tell Him that you love Him!

God often speaks loudest when we're quietest.

—Mark Batterson, *Whisper: How to Hear the Voice of God*

4

WHERE DOES GOD SPEAK TO YOU?

Where does God speak to you?

1. God can speak to you anywhere.

God is not limited by time or space. He can give a prophetic word about someone even before he is born (for example, King Cyrus in Isaiah 45:1-5). God planned for King Cyrus to help build the temple even before God created him in his mother's womb (Ezra 1:1-2).

You could be in an inconvenient place when God speaks to you. You could perhaps be in the bathroom or even attending an important appointment or meeting. At such times, it is easy to either ignore what He is saying or dismiss it as your imagination. The fact is, as His Word says that there is nowhere you can flee from His presence (Psalm 139:7-9). This means that wherever you may be, you can call upon Him and when you are ready to hear Him, He will speak to you.

2. He speaks to you when you are looking at His creation.

Listen to what the Psalmist says in Psalm 19:1-4: *"The heavens declare the glory of God; the skies proclaim the work of his hands. Day after day they pour forth speech; night after night they display knowledge. There is no speech or language where their voice is not heard. Their voice goes out into all the earth, their words to the ends of the world."*

Whenever you feel sad or lonely, just look around at God's creation, and you will surely realize that you are not alone in this universe. Creation is God's beautiful handiwork and speaks of His wondrous nature. Therefore, be comforted that God is around you—and He will speak to you through His creation.

3. God may ask you to go to another place before He speaks to you.

Sometimes the place where God normally speaks to you may become so familiar that you may take it for granted and "miss" it when He speaks to you. An example is when God told Jeremiah to go to the potter's house. *"This is the word that came to Jeremiah from the LORD, 'Go down to the potter's house, and there I will give you my message"* (Jeremiah 18:2).

Why did the Lord tell Jeremiah to go all the way to the potter's house instead of speaking to him where he was? Again, in Jeremiah 19:1-2, God told Jeremiah to buy a potter's clay jar and take some elders and senior priests to go out to the valley of Ben Hinnom and there he was to proclaim the words He wanted Jeremiah to say. Why didn't God speak to Jeremiah at the place where he was, instead of sending him to a different place on both occasions? Here you see God using "visual impact" at the potter's house and the smashing of the clay jar—to cause Jeremiah to understand what He was saying and the gravity in His words of warning to the people.

Sometimes, for instance, God may instruct you to go to another country to attend a seminar, and there He uses somebody to give you a prophetic word. Why does God want you, at some great expense sometimes, to travel to another place when He could have easily spoken to you at your home? One reason could be that you can get to a place of complacency in your familiar surroundings, where you begin to take Him for granted, and then your expectation begins to wane! God sometimes jolts you out of the sense of complacency and familiarity with Him, so that your sensitivity to His voice can become "heightened" when you are in an unfamiliar place.

4. God can transport you to another place before He speaks to you.

In Ezekiel 37:1-14, God transported Ezekiel and set him in the middle of a valley full of bones. God brought Ezekiel to this place, so He could teach him about prophesying to the dry bones. He could have shown him a picture of the dry bones or told him to prophesy over the dry bones without having to bring him to the middle of the valley. This is certainly a more effective method of using the visual form of vivid images which had a greater impact on Ezekiel. This, in turn, helped him understand God's message of hope for the people of Israel by actually seeing the "revival of the dry bones" and the power of prophesying.

5. God can speak to you while you are seeing a vision.

God may speak to you in a vision. Sometimes He may transport you to another place in the vision. You find an example in Daniel 8:2 where Daniel saw in the vision that he was in the citadel of Susa and he was able to observe what was happening in Susa.

6. God can speak to you when you are running away and hiding from your enemy.

In 1 Kings 19:9, God spoke to Elijah while he was in the cave, even though in the wilderness Elijah had asked God to take his life. God did not respond to Elijah but instead sent an angel to feed him in order to strengthen him so he would have the strength to travel forty days and night to Horeb (1Kings 19:4-8). God then spoke to Elijah when he was in the cave in Horeb and told him to go back to where he came from (1 Kings 19:11-15).

7. God can speak to you when you are indoors or outdoors.

God spoke to Balaam when he was outside riding his donkey (Numbers 22:30). God spoke to Samuel when he was in his bedroom (1 Samuel

3:8-9). He can also speak to you when you are asleep (Joel 2:28). God spoke to Jonah when he was sitting under a tree (Jonah 4:6). God spoke to Isaiah when he was worshipping in the temple (Isaiah 6:1-7). God spoke to Peter when he was praying on the roof (Acts 10:9-15).

8. God can speak to you in any noisy environment.

I used to think that I needed to go to a quiet place before I could hear God speak. Initially, when you are learning to hear His voice, it is beneficial to go to a quiet place to hear from Him. This helps you to shut out any other noise and distraction. However, one day the heavenly Father spoke to me regarding this. He said, "If you are so used to hearing My voice only in quiet places, then does this mean I cannot use you to minister to people in a noisy shopping center because you cannot hear My voice in the midst of the noise?" That really got me thinking. It is true that I am used to ministering to people in a church setting or to Christians. God's word and His love shine the brightest in dark places, so if I am to go to such dark places, I must train myself in such a way that I can hear His voice there as well. The Holy Spirit started to train me to hear God's voice, even in the midst of noisiness or in unfamiliar places.

Whenever I am invited to go to a Christian group to teach the members how to hear God's voice, I ask the leader for the names of the members, as I wish to seek God for a prophetic word for each one of them. Often, I will go to another room away from any distracting noises to seek God for a prophetic word for them. I have recently trained myself to quiet my spirit before the Lord even in a noisy environment by shutting out all the external noise and tuning into the frequency of God's voice. In fact, while commuting on the train on my way to work, I often seek God for prophetic words and type them on my mobile phone. I am grateful to God for His love and faithfulness for His people—and for giving me the boldness to speak out on His behalf. From the positive feedback I have received, I feel so blessed and encouraged that God's prophetic word truly ministered to them—and, I am happy to be used as God's conduit.

Prayer

Dear God, I thank You that You know my coming in and my going out and You know me intimately. I thank You that I can speak to You anywhere and that no location can limit Your ability to answer me or to have a conversation with me. I am so thankful that You can speak to me anywhere. Please help me be sensitive to Your voice so that wherever I am and even in the noisiest environment, I can tune in to Your voice. In Jesus' precious name. Amen.

Activation exercises

1. Ask God a question when you are driving. Wait and see, hear, and sense whatever thoughts come to your mind.

2. When you are on a train to work or when you are having your lunch break, type a question that you wanted to ask God on your mobile phone. Type whatever thoughts come to your mind.

3. Ask God a question when you are at home vacuuming the floor. Wait and see, hear and sense whatever thoughts come to your mind.

4. Ask God a question when you are going for a walk. Wait and see, hear and sense whatever thoughts come to your mind.

5. Ask God a question when you are cooking dinner. Wait and see, hear and sense whatever thoughts come to your mind.

SUMMARY

God can speak to you anywhere and you can speak to Him anywhere. He does not speak to you only when you are in church. He can speak to you even in a noisy environment. Sometimes He may bring you out from your familiar environment to speak to you because you have become so used to the familiar that you miss His voice. You must learn to be sensitive to hear Him speak to you anywhere.

Listen to God's voice in everything you do and everywhere you go. He's the one that will keep you on track.

—*Proverbs 3:6 (MSG)*

5
WHAT DOES GOD WANT TO SPEAK TO YOU ABOUT?

There is an innate curiosity among those who have never heard God's voice about what He wants to speak to them about. You may have come from a broken family where there was little communication happening. You may have grown up in your family feeling ignored. You may sometimes feel as though you are just a number in this wide world and that even if you cease to exist tomorrow, no one will even notice that you have departed from this earth. It is with this feeling of low self-esteem and lack of direction and purpose that you may feel surprised to hear that there is a God who wants to speak to you. Not only that, He wants to speak to you about the smallest details in your life and is interested in you, not because He wants something from you, but because He wants to give you purpose in your life.

What does God want to speak to you about?

1. God wants to speak to you about anything and everything that concerns your life.

God wants to speak to you about anything that you are concerned about, anything that interests you, or any issues that you are facing in your life. This includes speaking to you about your future, your destiny, your life assignment, His love for you, things He wants you to change, your health, family, marriage, life partner, dreams, fears, worries, career, and financial issues. The list is endless. He particularly longs to share with you His dreams for you. In a nutshell, He wants to speak to you about anything and everything, but only if you invite Him and allow Him into your life. He is a gentleman and will never force Himself into your life if you don't want Him there. In Revelation 3:20, Jesus said that He stands at the door and knocks and if you hear His voice and open the door, He will come in and dine with you and you with Him. Imagine Jesus, the King of Kings and the Lord of Lords, sitting at your dining table and talking to you! Yes, He will do this if you invite Him. He lets you have the choice of inviting Him in, even though He is all-powerful, and He can just speak, and the door will open for Him.

There are many examples in the Bible that show the different facets of your life in which God is interested. Some examples are:

1. He wants you to know that He loves you and that you are always in His thoughts (Psalm 139:17-18).
2. He wants you to know that when you trust and acknowledge Him, He will direct your path (Proverbs 3:5-6).
3. He wants to speak to you about the plans He has for your life (Jeremiah 29:11).
4. He wants to tell you that you are never alone and that His love for you is everlasting to everlasting (Joshua 1:5; Jeremiah 31:3).
5. He wants to speak to you about His grace, which is more than sufficient for you and that His power is made perfect in your weakness (2 Corinthians 12:9).
6. He wants to speak to you about accomplishing impossible things for Him because with Him all things are possible (Luke 1:37).
7. He wants to speak to you about your fears and He wants to tell you that His perfect love for you casts out all fear (1 John 4:18).
8. He wants to speak to you about casting your cares on Him for

He will carry your burdens for you daily (Psalm 68:19; Psalm 55:22).
9. He wants to speak to you about hope and remind you that when there seems to be no hope, He is the God of hope (Romans 15:13).
10. He wants to speak to you about the temptations you are facing and to tell you that He is faithful and that He will not allow you to be tempted beyond what you are able, but He will provide a way to escape so you can endure it (1 Corinthians 10:13).
11. He wants to speak to you about His comfort and that He is able to comfort you in all your afflictions and that your comfort is abundant through Christ (1 Corinthians 1:3-5).
12. He wants to speak to you about your disappointments and remind you that when you put your hope in Him, you will never be disappointed or be put to shame (Psalm 25:3; Romans 10:11; Isaiah 49:23).
13. He wants to speak to you about your confusion and to remind you that He is not a God of confusion but of peace (1 Corinthians 14:33).
14. He wants to tell you He will guide you until your last day on earth (Psalm 48:14).
15. He wants to speak to you about your finances and that He has promised you will succeed in everything you do and that He will prosper the works of your hands (Deuteronomy 30:9).
16. He wants to speak to you about your health and tell you He has given you good health because He has taken away all your diseases (Psalm 103:3).
17. He wants to speak to you when you experience anxiety concerning your children, that He, Himself, will teach your children (Isaiah 54:13).
18. He wants to speak to you about His joy, which will be your strength (Nehemiah 8:10).
19. He wants to speak to you about His peace for He has given you His peace that the world cannot give or take away and

that He will grant you peace in every circumstance (John 14:27; 2 Thessalonians 3:16).
20. He wants to speak to you about His love for you that extends to the heavens and His faithfulness that reaches to the skies (Psalm 36:5).

In a nutshell, God wants to speak to you regarding every area of your life and about all your concerns. The reason is that He loves and cares for you. You are the apple of His eye. God did not just create you and then leave you on this earth to fend for yourself. He was concerned about your well-being. Even before we're born, He had already written the plans for your life and He will never leave you. He has good and perfect plans for you (Jeremiah 29:11) and no plans of the enemy can thwart His plans for you (Job 42:2)!

2. He wants to speak to you about how the impossible can become possible.

Do you sometimes feel that you have hit a brick wall when praying for the salvation for someone or for a backslidden Christian to come back to the fold, or for God's intervention in an impossible situation? Perhaps you've been telling yourself "This is impossible! It's not going to happen!" However, didn't God say in the Bible, *"Is there anything too hard for Me?"* (Genesis 18:14, Jeremiah 32:27). You can ask God to show you a vision of the outcome and the positive results in these impossible situations. You may see a beautiful vision of the person receiving God's salvation and the joy on that person's face or you can see a vision of the backslidden person attending church again.

Many years ago, I was praying for my mom before she had her triple bypass heart surgery. I prayed that God would preserve her life as she had not accepted Him as her personal Savior. The heavenly Father showed me a vision of my mom singing in her dialect the following lyrics: "Believing in Jesus is so good, and He will save your soul." When I had that vision from the heavenly Father, I knew without a doubt that nothing would happen to my mom because she had not given her heart to God yet and that God would definitely save her soul. I felt comforted as peace reigned in my heart knowing that mom would be well after the surgery. The Holy Spirit also impressed upon my heart to pray that God Himself would perform the heart operation on my mom. My mom was out of the hospital in record time. A friend of mine later told me that her husband, who was much younger than my mom, had the same operation, but spent a longer period of recovery in the hospital. I truly believe God's hand was on my mom!

3. He wants to speak to you about performing inner healing in your life.

When God wants to perform inner healing in your life, He may bring someone to help you. That person may ask the Holy Spirit to bring you back to the memory of when you were hurt emotionally. You may be asked to see with your spiritual eyes what Jesus was saying or doing when you were going through that traumatic experience. You will most probably be able to see what Jesus was doing and saying in the screen of your mind. In this way, Jesus brings you the inner healing of memories and trauma, which sometimes many hours of counseling or prayer have not achieved. After your emotions are healed, you can then move on to fulfill the destiny that God has for you instead of being stuck in the same place. Sometimes during an inner healing session, you may not be able to see Jesus in your hurt memories, but you may be able to hear His voice, sense His presence, or feel His touch. Sometimes because of the trauma you have encountered, you may have shut off your physical eyes to see and this may also hinder you from seeing Him in the spiritual realm.

4. He wants to speak to you about removing the fear of your future.

God wants to speak to you when you are fearful of the future, unsure of what it holds for you, and especially when you are overwhelmed by setbacks in your life. He knows all about you and your future. He calls out to you, *"Come to me, all you who are weary and burdened, and I will give you rest"* (Matthew 11:28).

In late 2016, my son's job was made redundant. I fasted and prayed for him concerning this situation, and God showed me that Ben need not pound on every door for new employment opportunities. He had the matter under control, and He would direct Ben's path and a new door would open for him. The heavenly Father then gently asked me why I was behaving as if He was surprised at what had happened to Ben when He already knows what Ben's life will be like, even before he was born. As I received the Rhema word, I felt the burden lift off my shoulders. Two days after Ben's job was made redundant, we met up for lunch. I shared with him what God had impressed upon my heart about his situation. I declared in boldness and in faith that we were having a celebratory lunch to celebrate the end of one season and the beginning of a new season—as one door closes, God will open another! The prophetic word from God changed our worrisome perspective to one of comforting confidence.

Three months into 2017, nothing seemed to have changed in my son's job situation, even though many encouraging prophetic words were spoken over him. I asked God why it was taking so long for the manifestation of the new job. He gave me this verse in Isaiah 30:15, "*In quietness and confidence shall be your strength.*" He then impressed upon me to pray for Ben for the next seven days. He brought to my mind Joshua and the Israelites marching around the wall of Jericho and not saying anything until the seventh day when they gave out a shout. I prayed and was confident that on the seventh day, after giving a shout for the plans of the enemy to collapse; I would see a change in Ben's job situation.

Nothing in the natural realm seemed to be happening—after about three weeks, still no job for Ben! I went back to God in prayer as I became anxious and began to worry. This time He showed a picture of me flying a kite and I was holding very tightly onto the string. I heard His gentle voice say to me, "Let go *COMPLETELY*." Then, I saw the word "COMPLETELY" appear in capital letters! I realized that though I had confessed that God was in control of the situation, I was still holding on to the situation. He also reminded me that Ben is *His* son and that He will take care of Him. He brought to my memory the baby dedication when Ben was two months old. I could see very vividly his baby face and the clothes he was wearing. My husband, Paul, and I have dedicated Ben to God, and we are just Ben's stewards. I realized I had to let go and surrender Ben and his job situation completely to God. Suddenly, I felt the burden lift off my shoulders and I was so glad that I didn't have to carry it anymore!

I believed in faith that, in the fullness of time, God would bring the best job for Ben. God is never too late nor too early, but He is always on time. He can make all things beautiful in His perfect timing. Not long after, Ben was offered a position that paid 40% more than his previous job. Praise God that only He and He alone could have performed this miracle!

When you are conversing with God, He can ask you questions too.

You need to remember that any conversation involves two-way communication. How boring it is if you are the only person doing all the talking, and you are not allowing God to speak back to you! Do you know that God can ask you questions, too? Though He already knows every thought you have, and He will not be surprised, you may be the one surprised by the answers you give Him. Sometimes you do not even know what is in your heart until you verbalize it.

Some questions that God may ask you are (He knows the answers, but He wants to hear it from you!):

1. My child, what do you know about Me?
2. My child, what are your deepest dreams and desires?
3. My child, what are your deepest fears and concerns?
4. My child, what are the things you have done that you wish you could undo?
5. My child, what are the things that have happened to you that you feel guilty or ashamed of?
6. My child, what are the strongholds/addictions you want Me to help you overcome?
7. My child, what do you think My thoughts are concerning you?

When God asks you these questions and you give Him your answers, you must make sure you do not just walk away without waiting for

Him to respond to your answers. The Lord will help you see and feel what He sees and feels. The heavenly Father desires you to be expectant, positioned, and ready to adjust to the moving of the Holy Spirit in your life. You must strive to live under the leading of the Holy Spirit and to set your mind to what the Holy Spirit desires. You must learn to walk in step with the Holy Spirit (Galatians 5:25) and be obedient and responsive to His leading. You will find that the more you respond to Him, the more sensitive you will become to the prompting of the Holy Spirit.

What are the questions that you can ask God?

One tip I have learned is that when you have a dialogue with God, you should ask open-ended questions instead of asking closed-ended questions that only require "yes" or "no" answers. You need to be daring enough to ask Him about anything and everything. He will not be offended or surprised by what you ask. God doesn't only want to answer your questions—although those are important—He also wants to have a deep, personal relationship with you. Below are some examples of questions that you can ask God:

1. Dear heavenly Father, what are the special giftings that You have given me?

2. Dear heavenly Father, how much do You love me.

3. Dear heavenly Father, what are the things I do that make You sad?

4. Dear heavenly Father, what are the things I do that make You smile and bring pleasure to You?

6. Dear heavenly Father, what are my greatest strengths and how can I use them for Your glory?

7. Dear heavenly Father, what are my deepest fears and weaknesses and how can You help me overcome them?

8. Dear heavenly Father, in which areas of ministry can I serve You best?

9. Dear heavenly Father, which area of my life have I not surrendered to You yet?

In fact, there are endless things you can ask Him about. However, do take time to ask God for help and wisdom for yourself, your family and friends as He leads and reveals to you what is in His heart. His heart is always for the lost. He loves the people who do not know Him yet and He desires for you to fulfill your destiny in being part of His end-time army to bring in the harvest of souls. Your heavenly Father has a destiny for you that is far greater than for your success. He wants all your blessings and giftings to be used to bless others and bring people into His kingdom.

What are the things that can you ask God about?

1. You can ask God about anything and everything.

Hearing from God is vital if you are to enjoy His eternal plan for your life. Listening to God is a decision which only you can make. God won't force you to choose His will, but He will do everything He can to encourage you to say "yes" to His ways. This means God wants to be involved in even the smallest details of your life. His Word tells you to acknowledge Him in all your ways, and He will direct your path (Proverbs 3:6). To acknowledge God is to care about what He thinks and to ask for His opinion.

You can speak to Him about anything that is on your mind as He is interested in every aspect of your life. You may think that God is only interested in spiritual things, so you speak to Him about only spiritual matters. You might think that you shouldn't talk to Him about your day-to-day affairs as He is not interested and doesn't have time for you. You may tend to converse with Him only about the "major" issues that you are facing. Sometimes you may have a mentality that you should not trouble God over trivial things or He will get impatient or angry with you. This is a lie of the enemy which he uses to blind you, so that you may never have an intimate relationship with God as He intends. In the natural, you have best friends whom you share everything with —your aspirations, dreams, fears, hopes, likes, dislikes, etc. How much more does your heavenly Father wants to be involved in every part of your life because He loves and cares for you?

You also need to realize that God is not interested in just having one-way communication with you. So, whenever God talks to you, it is important that you hear what He is saying too. You can respond to Him through your prayers or through journaling your response to Him. Sometimes, you might not be bothered to hear His responses. He does not treat you like a robot where you take orders from Him. You are not His slave but His child. He does not want you to treat Him like an instant vending machine where you only want answers to your questions but are not interested in anything else about Him. Many of us see the heavenly Father as someone who supplies our needs and fulfills our desires. Few of us ever ask Him about the things that break His heart or His thoughts about certain situations. I suppose for most of us, we are so wrapped up on our own world of "me, me, me" that we never think of what is in His heart. Many of us live by existing just for ourselves and focusing on what we want and what we need all the time.

The privilege of being His child is that you can know the things that move His heart. He wants to share His heart's secrets with you if you take the time to ask Him. When you see someone in need or with a health issue, do you pause and ask God what He wants you to say to this person on His behalf? I believe that you will fall in love more and more with the heavenly Father when you go about doing the things that are on His heart. I like the song "Closer" by Bethel Music which has the lyrics about knowing God's heart, asking God to pull us a little closer and to take us a little deeper because we want to know His heart.

2. You can ask God about your health and other fears.

Many of us may have many health fears and other fears. When you take the time to speak to the heavenly Father about your fears and wait for His reply, He may remind you that His perfect love will cast out all fear and that He has not given you a spirit of fear and timidity, but of power, love, and self-discipline (2 Timothy 1:7). Many people live with fear their whole lives and sometimes these fears overwhelm them so much that they need to see a doctor or a psychiatrist. However, only God can show you when the fear first came into your life and only He can deliver you from all your fears. You don't need to spend lots of money speaking with people who can't really help you about your fear. You may end up being prescribed medicine to overcome your fear, but it will never help you in the long term.

God is the perfect person to talk to about your health fears for He is the one who created your body. Tell Him about any concerns you may have, about any aspect of your health. For example, if you have high blood pressure, you can ask Him questions such as, "God, can you please tell me when this high blood pressure came into my life? Was there a trigger that caused this to happen to me?" He can show you the root cause of the health issue if you ask Him. Maybe you've had unforgiveness towards someone and this may have caused a blockage in your heart. This, in turn, may have manifested as high blood pressure in your physical body. Some sicknesses are related to unforgiveness so instead of spending money to see a doctor and having to be on medication for life, how much better it would be if you first ask Him about the root cause and act on what He tells you to resolve this health issue.

Someone I knew had a high blood pressure condition. He sought God for a natural cure for this condition. He shared that God showed him what he should eat so as to reduce high blood pressure. When he ate what God showed him, his blood pressure went back to normal, and he did not need to take high blood pressure medications anymore. Your health problems could be related to diet, so have you ever thought of asking the heavenly Father what you should/should not eat to resolve the health problems?

Once I was ministering to a group of ladies at a women's retreat. As I was waiting on the Lord for a corporate word for them, the heavenly Father showed me that many of the ladies believed the lies of the enemy about their health, especially in hereditary sicknesses passed down from their parents. Many of them confessed what the doctors had told them about their health condition. For example, the doctor could say, "Since your parents have high blood pressure and diabetes, you will most likely also have this medical condition or be at risk of having these in the future." From what they have received from the doctor, many of them have declared this over themselves (even before any of the high blood pressure or diabetes appear in their body!) and tell everyone, "My parents have high blood pressure and diabetes, so I will most probably have high blood pressure and diabetes." You can probably guess what ailment they have in the years to come. You are right; they end up having high blood pressure and diabetes. Life and death are in the tongue's power (Proverbs 18:21). What you speak and believe will manifest. How much better to speak what the Bible says about your health instead of what the doctor says about your health! During the meeting, I taught them how to declare what God says about their health, and I also encouraged them to ask God to show them a vision of them in good health and enjoying the things that they love to do.

An example of "what you speak is what you get" is portrayed in the story about the Shunammite woman in 2 Kings 4:18-26. Her son had died. But when Elisha sent his servant to ask her, "Is it well with the child?" She answered, "It is well." She did not look at the circumstance, but she looked to the man of God who could raise her son from the dead (2 Kings 4:29-37).

3. You can speak to God about your finances.

Another area you can speak to the heavenly Father is about your finances. Many people have not asked Him before they invest (i.e. what, where, when, how to invest). Many of us may live under the curse of debt, yet we have not asked the heavenly Father how to get out of debt. Dr. Mark Virkler (from Communion with God Ministries) said his mother told him to study for two degrees in case he didn't earn enough to support himself as a minister. It became a curse in his life, for he was always living in lack until God revealed this to him. He was able to break this curse over his life.

Sometimes you can also put a curse on yourself regarding finances. You may have confessed the following: "I never have enough money to live on and I live from payday to payday." Guess what? You will not have enough money for "as you speak, so it is." I love what my Nigerian friend, Bukky, said about how the Nigerians select good names for their children. For example, her husband's name is Olufemi which means "God loves me" and her name is Oluwabukunola which means "God has added to my wealth." Their daughter's name is Oluwabukunayomi which means "God has added to my joy" and their son's name is Oluwaferanmi which means "God loves me." What a wonderful heritage to give to their children. What they have done is so biblical, as God often uses a specific name to give identity to a person.

In Genesis 17:5, God changed the name Abram (noble father) to Abraham (father of many) and in Genesis 17:15, God changed Sarai's name (princess) to Sarah (mother of nations). In Genesis 32:28, God changed Jacob's name (liar, cheat, usurper) to Israel (God fights; having the power of God). Can you imagine being called a liar and a cheat every day by your parents and friends? But imagine each time you hear your name being called, and it means you "have the power of God." How can this person not fulfill his destiny according to his name?

I used to struggle with finances and having enough because I come from a poor family. My parents struggled to put enough food on the table to feed ten children. When we had our meals, there wasn't much conversation, because we were busy grabbing the food to put on the plate, because if you were too slow, you ended up with no food. I grew up having this "poverty and lack" mentality. I asked the Lord: "How can I get out of this mentality?"

One day, during worship in the church, God showed me a picture of a cake that was cut into ten pieces. He asked me this pertinent question: "If you take two pieces of cake and give it to others, how many pieces of cake are left?" Immediately I said, "eight pieces." He gently told me, "In the natural, this is correct and logical. However, in My kingdom's economy, even when you give away two pieces of cake, and even if you give away the whole cake, I can multiply and give you more cakes than what you had at the beginning. I am trying to teach you to not be afraid to sow financially into My kingdom for when you give away what I have asked you to give, I can give you even more than what you started with. Live in My kingdom's economy and you will never need to fear financial lack in your life again!" This is a precious lesson which the heavenly father has taught me. Even as a mature Christian, when I give to the Lord, at the back of my mind, I think, *I have $40 in my wallet so now that I have given $20 to the Lord, I have $20 left.* The heavenly Father is teaching me that His kingdom's economy does not work in this way. He can multiply money at any time. He can put money in my wallet and my bank account at any time. I have heard of testimonies where people owing the bank money have gone to the bank to pay the debt, only to find that the bank had no record of their debt. God erased the loan from the bank system! If God can do this for His other children, He can do this for us too!

God's love for me knows no bounds. He has to keep on reminding me about the key principles of His kingdom's economy. This is because sometimes the message does not seem to get through to me. Over time, I may forget about what He says about His kingdom's economy. On my recent holiday trip to Osaka, Japan, I was walking along a pathway with my brother-in-law and my husband, Paul. We had to walk in single file along the narrow path. My brother-in-law walked in front of me and my husband walked behind me. As my brother-in-law passed a certain laneway, there was a sudden gust of wind and a piece of paper blew in front of me (Normally, I would not pay any attention to a paper blowing onto my path). However, when I looked at the piece of paper, I saw the word "1000." When I picked up the paper, I realized that this was a $1,000 yen (which is equivalent to A$12). After I picked this up, I could distinctly hear the heavenly Father's voice speaking. He said, "My daughter, why are you so worried about finances? Just as I have caused the wind to blow the $1000 yen in front of you, I can do the impossible for you in the area of finance. I am not limited by anything or by any economy." Wow, this really blew me away, that the heavenly Father was speaking so gently to me about financial fears. I know that whenever I have any concerns about finances, I will always remember this incident. I have kept the $1000 yen as a memento and as a reminder that He can perform a financial miracle in my life. I am waiting for Him to perform the miracle of me being able to sow $5 million into the mission field. I know that this dream will definitely come to pass!

WHAT DOES GOD WANT TO SPEAK TO YOU ABOUT? 83

When I was looking for an editor for this book, I had two quotes for the project. One of them was cheaper but not a Christian, the other gave a higher quote but is a Christian. As I was on a tight budget, using my human thinking, I decided to go with the cheaper quote (as most of us would do). However, after informing the Christian editor and telling her that I would not be going ahead with her, I felt an uneasiness. I sensed that I was using my human reasoning to make the decision. I decided to spend time asking God why I had an uneasy feeling. As I surrendered the book to him as an offering, He began to tell me that He wanted me to go with the Christian editor because He wanted to bless her with this project, and He was blessing her through me. He wanted to use this blessing to show her how much He loves and cares for her and to let her know that she had not made the wrong decision in starting the business. In obedience, I changed my decision and went with the Christian editor. After I did that, His peace flooded over me, and I knew that I made the right decision.

My friend, Serene Huang, gave me the prophetic word regarding my decision. The prophetic word was: "The money will come in. The money and blessing will be returned back to you many folds." What a loving God we serve who cares for all His children and is able to use one child to bless another child because we are all in the same family of God. Even though in the end, she decided to not go ahead with the project, I was glad that I was obedient to God, no matter what the outcome was. God in his goodness provided me with another Christian editor.

Concerning obedience in giving, Reverend Dominic Yeo, Senior Pastor of Trinity Christian Centre, Singapore shared in his book, *Potential to fulfillment*, how God impressed upon his heart to give all that he had when he was attending a conference on intercession in Guatemala. This is what he wrote:

> *I was taken aback by the way people were giving, not only their money, but shoes, rings, watches, and even clothing! Now, you have to understand that I was merely attending this great conference and the money that I had with me was the cash*

advance that I have taken from my church for my stay in Guatemala. Hence, I was not thinking about making any offerings. All the while, I was telling God that the money that I had was not mine and that I had no intention of parting with it. As I got closer to the huge sack before me, I heard an internal voice telling me to empty all the money that I was carrying into the sack. A big debate went on in my head but before I could reach any conclusion, I found myself staring at a smiling usher. I obeyed the Lord, taking every single note of the church money that I was carrying and putting into the sack. And then, as I turned around to return to my seat, God asked me to remove my shoes. Now, I was really starting to argue with God. I told Him that I needed my shoes to walk back to the hotel. But God was not interested in my shoes. Rather, it was what I had put into my shoes—more money. Out of obedience a second time, I emptied my shoes, shirt pocket, and pants of all the money I had on me. All this time, I was wondering how I would get by for the next few days. Yet, I still returned to my seat with joy in my heart. All of a sudden, the internal voice returned, and I distinctly heard it resound inside me, "Son, open your wallet." My immediate response was, "Lord, I emptied my wallet for you and there is nothing in there!" But the unmistakable voice of God urged me to look into my wallet. Following the prompting, I opened my wallet, and I saw money in it! I instinctively reached into my shirt pocket, pants and shoes and found dollar notes in them as well! I experienced such a surge of faith that day, knowing that when I acted in pure obedience to His voice, I had broken into a new realm of miracles. Therefore, to seal my faith and to remind me that I can trust Him and take that extreme measure of faith, I kept a US$100 note from that conference to this day. It is a token of reminder for me, to help me remember my faith experience. To this day, whenever I am challenged in faith, I take out this note and remember His goodness and this wonderful miracle. It continues to inspire me to trust God for His miraculous provision, be it for my family, or for the church when I was involved in the church building program.

4. You can speak to God regarding which ministry He wants you to sow into.

There are many ministries that require finances to operate and therefore these ministries prayerfully encourage people to sow financially into them. My former pastor gave the advice that when we sow, we must sow into good soil so that it will yield a great harvest. As we are stewards of the finances that God has put into our hands, we must have the discernment from the Lord on which ministries to sow into.

My friend, Serene Huang, shared this testimony regarding how God directed her to sow into a particular ministry:

> *When I stepped into the mission field, working amongst the poorest of the poor, the widows and the orphans, it felt so much like a home-coming to me. When you are amid your calling, it always feels perfectly right. Later, moving to Perth, Western Australia I founded Global Mission United and became one of its Mission Directors. Being the founder and the Mission Director, I receives a floodgate of daily appeals seeking our partnership. But unless I sense the Holy Spirit prompting, I have learned not to move until He tells me to. It usually comes as a gentle stirring in my innermost being, in my spirit-man. The greater the demand of the ministry, the greater my dependency on the gift of discernment, and the greater the need to daily hear from God and allow Him to lead me. Two weeks ago, I received one of the many mission videos sent to Global Mission United. It featured an orphanage like many others, with children happy and smiling. One afternoon I felt the Holy Spirit say to me, 'I would like you to bless this orphanage.' I have never met the pastor nor know anyone there, so I contacted the gentleman who sent the video to me. At the very hour that I received the prompting, the pastor of the orphanage was desperately crying out to the Lord, as in the last week there was no food on the*

table for the children. Being located in an anti-Christian community, the local authority ordered that many surveillance cameras be installed within twenty-four hours around the orphanage. This added to the stress of his already empty food supply (empty jar). By the prompting of the Holy Spirit, the Lord was about to fill up the jar of this orphanage with oil (1 Kings 17:12-16). The Lord said to me, 'Upon this land where the orphanage stands, I am going to send forth a stream of living water. The children shall drink of it and never will they thirst again.' So, with this prophetic word that was received from the Lord, funds were released to this ministry. Connections were made and under the prompting of the Holy Spirit, Global Mission United was able to respond to the need and be used in lifting the name of Jesus Christ. Ministry is about the people on God's heart. I have learned to lean heavily on the prompting of the Holy Spirit, to discern, to hear and to be guided by the 'compass' of His voice. Radical generosity guards our hearts against the love for this world.

Recently I asked Joel Chelliah, Senior Pastor from Centrepoint Church in Perth about how he discerns which ministries the church should partner with. This is what he shared:

> *I get a lot of invites to participate and partner with many organizations. That tends to happen when your church starts to grow. People from mission organizations target you as the senior pastor and try to win you over. But for me, after sitting in a lot of meetings and talking to a lot of different people, I find that when something calls me to partner, it leaps in my spirit and I feel like we have to do something to help. There is this urgency for us to really rise up and do something. And that is usually when I feel God calling us to do something; we feel like we have to contribute, we have to add our voice to the choir. We have to add our hands to the toil. That's when I feel that we have to partner. Something I feel in my spirit. This is not always the case, even though there are good ministries and good missionary*

organizations out there. I choose not to partner with everybody. I just choose to partner with those that I feel a strong burden from God calling us to get involved with.

5. You can speak to God about the salvation of your loved ones and friends.

All of us are concerned about the salvation of our loved ones and friends. Sometimes we pray and pray, but nothing seems to happen at all. We may find it easy to give up after a while. We would not have given up if we had asked God to speak to us on how we could pray for them or asked Him to give us a picture of our loved ones when they come to the Lord.

My eldest brother, Charles, was diagnosed with stage four esophagus cancer four years ago. I cried to God to save his soul. I remembered distinctly that I was in a stadium for an evangelistic meeting that week after hearing the distressing news about my brother's illness. As I was early, I sat in the stadium and interceded for my brother. As I interceded for my brother, I distinctly heard the heavenly Father speak to me. He said, "My son, Jesus, loves Charles so much that He will leave the ninety-nine sheep in the fold to go and search for this lost sheep, Charles." He then showed me a picture of Him holding Charles in the palm of His hands and telling me that His hands are upon Charles. When I received the word and the vision, it gave me so much comfort and encouragement to continue to pray for his salvation. I knew it would happen because God's words will not return to Him void but will accomplish what He desires and achieve the purpose for which God sent it (Isaiah 55:11).

God can also show you any strongholds in the minds of your loved ones or friends that prevent them from coming to the Lord. God can reveal the veil that is stopping them from knowing Him. One day as I was praying for my brother and asking God to reveal the strongholds preventing him from coming to the Lord, I heard the word, "Freemasonry." Immediately, I called my sister-in-law, Cynthia, to find out whether my brother had ever been involved with Freemasonry. She confirmed that he had. With this revelation, I prayed against this stronghold with confidence. Within a short time, my brother Stewart was sharing with Charles from Luke 23:39-43 about how one thief was saved on his dying day. Charles resisted because he wanted God to heal him first before he would believe in Jesus. However, after Stewart shared further, he accepted Jesus as his personal Savior. Praise the Lord!

So, when God shows you the strongholds in your unsaved loved ones, you can then strategically intercede and make targeted intercession that is precise and effective in pulling down their strongholds. You want to hit the bullseye when you intercede for your unsaved loved ones, instead of shooting your arrows of intercession everywhere and hoping that one arrow will strike the bullseye. God knows what experiences your unsaved loved ones and friends have gone through and He can reveal it to you. He can also let you know when your unsaved loved ones and friends are ready to accept the salvation message. You do not need to keep on sowing and digging but when you hear the heavenly Father's voice concerning their salvation, you will know it's time. You will know how, when, and where to prepare and soften the ground of their hearts and also when to reap and what to say. Evangelism with the help of the Holy Spirit is not burdensome. *God is patient towards those who do not know Him and is not willing that any should perish, but that all should come to repentance* (2 Peter 3:9).

6. You can speak to God about your children.

Another area you can speak to God is about your children. Do you know that as much as your children are yours, they belong to God? When my son was in high school, he was having some difficulties with some of his school subjects. I brought my prayer request to God daily. One day, He told me, "Ben is also My son and I care about him. As much as you love him, you can never love him as much as I love him. I have great plans and future for his life, and he will fulfill each one of them. Leave him in My hands and do not stress about it anymore." A load was lifted off my shoulders when I heard from Him. I have shared this testimony with many parents who are also concerned about their children's studies. I empathize with them. Those parents whose children are high flyers in school can never really understand this feeling. I once asked someone during a group prayer meeting to keep my son in prayer as he had an exam that week. That person retorted, "You mean you need to pray for your son when he takes an examination? What is there to pray? You shouldn't need prayer concerning this area." The reason he thought it was unnecessary to pray regarding this matter was that all his children are high flyers in school and he never needs to worry about them not doing well. I learned on that day that when God allows me to go through difficult situations, it is so that with the same comfort and encouragement He has given me, I can comfort and encourage others who are going through the same situation.

You can converse with Him about anything in your heart. This includes even your deepest heartaches and pain. Adam and Jun gave me permission to include this testimony of how God comforted them with a prophetic vision of the future when they were going through some emotional pain:

> *After going through a miscarriage (1st pregnancy) and having emergency surgery for a gynecological condition, I was feeling hopeless about the prospect of being a mother. During one of our prayer sessions, Rinda encouraged me to listen/experience what the Lord had to say to me. Suddenly a vision came so vividly, and I saw a vision of me and a little boy (who looked like my husband!) standing in a garden looking at a pot of beautiful sunflowers. In this vision, I was teaching this little boy about sunflowers. I felt a sense of peace come over me, which is something I had not felt since having a miscarriage. Holding on to this vision gave me so much comfort when the situation seemed hopeless. When I became pregnant again, the memory of the vision helped keep me strong throughout the first trimester (I had previously miscarried at eleven weeks). Since then, I've had two beautiful children, a boy, and a girl. One day about three years later, my son (who is a mini version of my husband) and I were having a conversation and looking at a pot of sunflowers that we had planted together. Suddenly, God brought to my memory that this scene is exactly the same vision that He had given me three years earlier. It was an overwhelming moment*

knowing He has been so faithful, and His promise had come to fruition.

7. You can speak to Him about your career.

Have you ever thought of asking God about your career? Don't you think He is interested in this vital part of your life? When you apply for a job, you can ask Him to open or close the door. You can ask for a divine appointment so that you can know more about the company you are applying for. A few years ago, I was thinking of applying for a job in another company. As I was casually talking to a new colleague about this company, she told me she had worked in that company previously. She told me it was not a good place to work. It was as if God gave me an insight into this company and showed me that this company was not for me. However, I was still unconvinced, and, in my heart, I thought that I would still apply for that job. In His mercy, God closed the door in such a way that the position was closed before I could even apply for it. God is the one who knows the beginning and the end.

My son went for a job interview after he graduated from his Environmental Engineering course. For all intents and purposes, the interview went well. So, he was disappointed when he was not offered the job. A few months later, he heard that this company was not doing well and that they had subsequently made the person who was offered the position redundant. God had closed the door for my son in that company even though we were disappointed at the time that he did not get the job.

I also remember when my son was applying for an internship as part of his requirement before he could graduate from his course. The criteria for the internship were strict, particularly in terms of how much money must be paid to the student during the internship. Companies generally do not pay for most internships, and students are contented to be able to get an unpaid internship. This requirement was quite a lot of money for a company to pay. I prayed for him and God showed me a vision of a boat floating in the sea with no oars. I asked God why the boat had no oars and how would the boat be able to reach the shore at all? I heard God distinctly said to me, "Leave Ben's internship to Me. There is nothing you, Paul, or Ben can do. The boat without oars signifies that you can't get to the destination unless it is by supernatural means. Leave it with Me for I am the One that will bring the boat to the desired destination." Within a short period, God opened the door to a government department willing to pay the amount stipulated in the internship terms. There was only one position available. Praise God that they offered Ben that one and only internship in the government department. I have learned that many times when we surrender all the plans we have to our heavenly Father and not "try to help" Him, He can then take over and give us the best outcome. The spoken, personalized word of the Lord contains power, energy, and authority to sustain each of us during our Christian walk, especially when we are in the valley or in the desert.

In March 2019, I went for a job interview after resigning from my job four months earlier. This interview was for a job that I had not applied for, but my former manager had recommended the job to me. I asked various intercessors to pray for me. One intercessor, D.S., said she felt led to pray that "this place will not be one of striving, but where there will be rest in the midst of the work." When I was called for the second interview, I asked the intercessors to pray for me again. One of my friends, Sue B, said she saw a vision of a hand that fitted the glove exactly. Another friend, Serene Huang, said she saw three words, "It was given." Another intercessor, Tuan, saw a vision of me looking thrilled and walking away from the building with a piece of paper in my hand. Another friend, Pat L, who was praying for me three days before the interview, had this prophetic word for me, "You will be offered a job soon and you're to take it." Guess what, two hours later, after the second interview, they told me they were offering me the job! I was so blessed to have so many intercessors praying for me regarding this job.

8. You can speak to God about how He can use you to deliver strongholds from other people's lives.

God speaks to you when He wants to free people from the hold of demonic spirits. He will help you discern the spirit that is involved in that person's life so that they can be delivered from these strongholds. He will tell you what and when the door was opened that caused the demonic stronghold to enter that person's life. God can also tell you how the demonic spirit came in, for example, whether it was through the family line (refer to Deuteronomy 5:9), or by the person's own invitation. Sometimes, the demonic spirit may have entered the person when the person encountered trauma in his or her life. As there are various ways that spirits can gain access to a person's life, learning to listen to God's voice will help you be more effective when conducting deliverance sessions.

9. You can speak to God regarding your ministry.

Jesus first heard from the Father before He did or said anything. He did what He saw the Father doing (John 5:19). In every instance, Jesus presented Himself as a servant under orders from His Father. Even the Holy Spirit conforms to this same pattern of speaking what He hears from the Father (John 16:13). Hearing from God regarding ministry is the pattern even for the Spirit of God. It should also be the pattern for your life as well. The Holy Spirit may speak to individuals, telling them where to go and what to do (Acts 8:29, 10:19-20). The Holy Spirit can hinder or forbid where ministry is concerned (Acts 16:6-7). The Holy Spirit may compel a person to go to a certain destination (Acts 20:22). Many obedient men and women of God have answered the call to ministry when God called them. Their obedience in heeding the voice of God has impacted many souls for the kingdom of God. I am so glad that these men and women of God were obedient to step out in faith and trust in God. He enabled them to accomplish the assignment that He had given them. It starts with them hearing the voice of God and obeying and taking the step of faith. Below are some giants of faith whose testimonies showed how much each one of them can fulfill the good works that God has prepared for them when they obeyed His voice.

Reverend Naomi Dowdy in her book *Destiny Calling* wrote:

> *Among the churches where I ministered in Singapore was Trinity Christian Centre, a small church I found to be 'dead.' In*

my opinion, the worship and prayer at that time were lifeless. As I walked out of the church, I muttered under my breath, 'Thank You, Jesus, I don't ever have to come back to this church again!' I had never said those words before in my life and I have not said them since, but at that moment, those were my honest feelings!

When the Assistant General Superintendent of the Assemblies of God in Singapore was sharing about a visa problem with the current missionary pastor of Trinity, Reverend Naomi Dowdy shared that she heard the Holy Spirit say to her in an audible voice, "And you are going to take the church." Reverend Naomi Dowdy went on to become a Pentecostal woman leading the fastest growing church in Singapore (Trinity Christian Centre) and passed the baton to Reverend Dominic Yeo in March 2005 to take over Trinity Christian Centre as the Senior Pastor. If she had not heeded the voice of the heavenly Father, the destiny of Trinity Christian Centre may not have been fulfilled.

Recently I asked my senior pastor, Pastor Joel Chelliah from Centrepoint Church, Perth (Western Australia) how he and his wife, Pastor Sharon, started Centrepoint and why he chose Centrepoint as the church name. This is what he shared:

> *Sharon and I were serving in Life City Church under Pastor David Storer for about ten years as their children and youth pastor. We were very happy there, we loved the house where we grew up, got baptized there, filled with the Holy Spirit there, got married there and so we were very satisfied and happy to serve Pastor Storer. One particular day at about 3 or 4 in the morning, God spoke to me in a dream and showed me that Sharon and I would be planting a church. When I woke up in the middle of the morning, I immediately woke Sharon and said, 'I think God has been speaking to me and I think that God wants us to plant a church.' Her immediate response was, 'Yes I know,' because God had actually been speaking to her for a long period of time about getting ready to plant a church. At that point, we went to our senior pastor and we submitted it to him. He actually told us that he had been feeling the same way and that we had*

outgrown our shoes there. With tears, he blessed us, and sent us out with a wonderful team to plant Centrepoint Church. So that is how we found out—through a dream—and confirmed by our senior pastor as well. God also showed me the name for the church-plant. I saw a picture that our church would meet together, and the ripple effect of the house would go out far and wide. There would be a centre point of gathering where everyone came in but the impact of that gathering and the encounter with God would have far-reaching effects into the whole community. That is how we got the name 'Centrepoint' for our church.

I asked Pastor Cheng Lai, the founder of Faith Community Church in Perth, how he came to pastor the church. Below is his testimony:

> *I had always wanted to do some theological studies but could not do this in Singapore as I had to study full-time and therefore could not serve as a pastor simultaneously. After some research, I discovered that the West Australian Bible College in Perth could take overseas students on a part-time basis. In July 1995, when seeking God's confirmation about coming to Perth, I felt God speaks to me from Ezekiel 3:10-11: 'And he said to me, 'Son of man, listen carefully and take to heart all the words I speak to you. Go now to your people in exile and speak to them. Say to them, 'This is what the Sovereign Lord says,' whether they listen or fail to listen.' I firmly believed that was the word of the Lord for me to go to Perth to serve and to speak to our own people in exile (those who had emigrated to Australia).*
>
> *God also gave my wife, Ellen, a verse from Isaiah 54:2: 'Enlarge the place of your tent, stretch your tent curtains wide, do not hold back; lengthen your cords, strengthen your stakes.' We had previously bought a house in Perth so that pastors from Singapore could stay in it when they came for their holidays, but we now believed God wanted us to stay in that house and serve Him in Australia.*

> *When I came to Perth in January 1996, I visited two churches but as the church members were mainly Caucasians, I did not feel that these two churches were the place that I should serve. Some weeks later, someone invited me to The Church of Resurrection. After attending that church for about three weeks, I was asked to join their pastoral team and some six months later, I was asked to take over after their pastor stepped down.*
>
> *Whilst waiting for the Lord's confirmation to take on that responsibility, the Holy Spirit impressed upon me that I should take up that position for 'He has called me for such a time as this' (Esther 14b). That confirmation came after my quiet time and when I opened my eyes, I saw for the first time in my life a full double rainbow in the sky. My original intention was to come to Perth to study and not take over a church, but God had other plans. I set about to consolidate that church, by making radical changes which included changing the name to Faith Community Church Inc. By God's grace and enablement, Faith Community Church has grown to be a strong and vibrant community church today.*

Pastor Taryn Hamilton from Centrepoint Church, Perth, shared how she heard God's voice regarding going into full-time ministry:

> *I was offered a full-time role in the church. At first, I thought 'No way could I give up my job.' As I prayed to God and surrendered that opportunity to Him, He gave me an undeniable peace about following that path into ministry. I heard Him say, 'Trust and follow Me, I've never let you down so far.'*

Pastor Peter Hammer from Centrepoint Church, Perth, shared with me recently how God showed him a vision regarding going into full-time ministry:

> *The Holy Spirit oftentimes speaks to me through images and this is how He called me into church-based ministry. I'd invested my gap-year after high school into Bible college before starting in*

> *university. I loved the experience and soaked up all that I could in both theory-content and practical experience. By the end, it felt like this was something I'd love to do for the rest of my life. I was see-sawing between what I should study next and turned to prayer (the place I should have started at). God answered me with a picture of a large container ship heading out to sea through a series of buoys and after going quite some distance, it changed course turning ninety degrees. The interpretation soon followed that I would be called to the business world for a time that I was to pursue wholeheartedly. At some point though, God would change the course and after a season of transition, I would have my full attention on church-based ministry. This is exactly how things have unfolded. I graduated from university with a commerce degree and worked full time as a management accountant. Then for four years, I worked part-time in accounting and part-time in church before coming on church staff full-time in 2012.*

When my friend, Pastor Sabrina Chow, recently took the challenge to plant a church, Risen Christian Assembly in Singapore, it was through God telling her to do it. It was two years of preparation where God gave her the vision and the values for the church. There were many prophetic words that God had spoken to her previously. Though it may have seemed easier and more comfortable to stay where she was, she heeded the voice of the heavenly Father. God has already used her obedience to bring many people to salvation as she reaches out to the church's local community.

My friend Serene Huang shared with me recently how the Lord dropped "India" into her heart. This is her testimony of how God directed her about ministry in India:

> *The Lord dropped India in my heart, a country I'd never thought of. The moment He dropped that into the deep recesses of my spirit, from within me, it started to birth forth a desire from that which was in the supernatural realm into the natural world. It became an 'I know, and I know it will happen'*

experience. But nothing was going to happen, it seemed, for many years. Yet, for as many years as I waited, my words were those of faith. When asked where I was going, with no trips planned, I announced 'India.' The next question predictably followed, 'When are you going?' I had no answer. I just knew I was going. Later that year, I felt a push in my spirit to go to India. From that trip, many divine connections were established. But what God was trying to birth forth was a global platform to reach the lives of those who desperately need the gospel yet are untouched by its power.

A mission trip would be enough, I thought. I was thinking as Hannah, believing God for a son when God wanted to birth a prophet. It was greater than what I had thought or imagined. Upon returning, I felt there was more. God very quickly raised a team of men and women of a different spirit through Global Mission United. With that arrow pulled out of its quiver, Global Mission United launched its first team into India. Our team goes into the valleys and streets and walks amongst the broken, the destitute and the tired. Amid bleak hopelessness, we introduced Christ to them. One day, these sad faces will, with joy unspeakable, look us in the face and say, 'Because of you, we now know Jesus.' 2019 is the year that the Lord has prophetically given us 1500 children. I trust that there is a bigger picture, a grander story that God is weaving bit by bit into each day, each conversation, and each interaction. He looks at the people of India with such fond compassion, with the limitless love of a Father's heart. As we act in obedience and faith, God's plan for India will begin to form and be revealed to us. The things we do on earth for Christ will determine the greatness of our eternal destiny.

10. You can speak to God about your future life partner.

Many of you who are single are very interested and curious to know who your life partner will be. As you hear stories of abusive and loveless marriages, there are fears that you may end up with a "monster" as a life partner who will make your life a living hell. As children of a loving heavenly Father who always gives you the best, if you ask Him, He may let you have a glimpse of your future with your life partner. A Christian couple I know (James and Angela) shared how God brought them together even though they were living in two different countries. It's a very encouraging testimony and they have given me permission to share their testimonies in order to encourage those of you who are still seeking a life partner.

James shared the following testimony:

> *When I came to the Lord, I had an incredible desire to know His voice and to be led by His Holy Spirit. The one area I felt I needed guidance for was who I should marry as I understood that the Lord knew the best woman for me. I didn't want to marry someone whose calling was not compatible with mine. I learned to recognize the voice of the Lord early in my Christian walk, so as I met a potential candidate, I would ask God if this person was the one which He had chosen for me. However, His response was always a consistent 'No.' I kept on getting the same 'no' answer until I spent time in prayer and asked Him to speak to me about this huge area of concern. And He did! As I was spending time in prayer one day, God spoke to me from Genesis 24 about how Abraham had sent his servant to his father's house to search for a bride for his son Isaac. I understood that the Lord was speaking to me and He would be the one who would choose for me. She would be from a similar background. He also took me to Proverbs 31 and highlighted various characteristics of the one He had chosen for my life partner. I knew no one that would fit the description. It made me wonder how and when I would meet this person. Years went by and I heard the Lord respond with a familiar 'No' when I asked Him about an 'interesting' lady I'd meet. I was getting older and since there was no one in sight and no answer from heaven, this generated a great amount of anxiety in me.*
>
> *One evening I was out for a walk, looking up at the night sky,*

and seeing the small snowflakes fall on my face, I asked Him 'When, Lord, when?' At that moment, I heard the same still small voice assuring me He had things under control. There was a prophetic word 'red' given to me regarding my life partner which I understood to mean 'Chinese wedding.' This gave me a clue that she would be Chinese. God also gave me the prophetic words, 'Do not settle.' I had almost settled for one lady who kept showing up on my radar, but God showed me in a vision how I would be miserable if I chose her. Two years had gone by and I decided I would spend a few days in prayer to seek God about this matter. Eventually, a sister introduced me to an online introduction service (e-harmony) which I was reluctant to join. However, she insisted that I should try it out and helped me with the application process. After about two months, a match came up. The person lived in a different country and I only met her after sensing that the Lord was not resisting me in this. After meeting the woman, something assured me in my spirit that I had found the match I'd waited so long for—my Rebekah. She also fits the description that the Lord spoke to me about many years earlier. She was also an Australian-born Chinese. We have now been married for over four years. Glory to God!

Angela had the following testimony regarding how God led her to meet her life partner:

> I had been praying about my life partner for many years as this was an issue of great importance to me. However, despite various attempts at dating, it rarely felt right at some point, either for me or for the other party. As the years progressed, this issue became an increasing source of frustration and great unhappiness to me. In my low points, I had even thought perhaps I had missed out, and I queried God about why He hadn't made this happen for me yet. He knew my heart's desire; it was He who had created me. When I was the bridesmaid at my sister's wedding, I cried out to God, 'What about me?' I declared, 'God if you can do it for my sister, you can

do it for me too!' I also registered on the same online platform that my sister had used to find her life partner. My thinking was that I would do my part and God would do the rest. Anyway, the following month, James was one of my matches. When I first saw James' name and location from WA, I thought this was short for Washington or some faraway place in the States. However, much to my relief, I discovered that WA is Western Australia and that we had so much in common. The more I got to know him, the more I found him to have similar core values to me. James came to Hong Kong for a short visit and a break in February. When I saw him coming out of the airport, I felt in my spirit that he was the one, but I didn't want to jump the gun and run ahead of God. At the end of the trip and after he had returned to Australia, he decided to give 'us' a go. We went to Japan for a trip. Whilst on the bus trip, we made a stop at the supermarket and James wanted to buy some fruit. He said he wanted an orange. I suggested perhaps mandarin would be easier to peel for the bus trip, but James said he would like an orange because it was his favorite fruit. This was so significant because a few years earlier when I was doing quiet time, I asked God what my future husband's favorite fruit was. God answered 'orange.' I wrote this down in my journal (three to four years before I even met James!) This was a confirmation on the trip that James was the partner He had chosen for me. In my heart of hearts, I had wanted someone who was Australian-born-Chinese and a Christian. God knows my innermost thoughts and desires, even when I don't say it out loud.

From the testimonies of James and Angela, we can see that God loves you so much that He has prepared someone special for you and that He knows your deepest thoughts and desires. What a loving heavenly Father He is to you! God has already told you to come boldly to the throne of grace, that you may obtain mercy and find grace to help you in your time of need (Hebrews 4:16). You can, therefore, be bold and ask God any questions that pertain to your life.

Prayer

Dear heavenly Father, I never realized that there are so many areas in my life that You are interested in and that You want to speak to me about. Forgive me for my wrong assumption that You are not interested in me and You have nothing much to say to me. There are so many questions I have about my relationships, career, finances, etc., but I never realized that I can ask You about them. Help me never to be afraid to speak to You regarding what is in my heart. Help me to surrender my life to You for I know that You are such an intimate Father who wants to guide me in every major decision of my life. Help me to ask You what is in Your heart. From today onwards, I want to let You show me/tell me what is in Your heart for me and for others who have yet to know You. In Jesus' name. Amen.

Activation exercise

1. Dear heavenly Father, can you please tell me/show me/let me sense one thing that is stopping my loved ones/friends (name one of them) from coming to know and accept You? (Write down what He shows you.)

2. Dear heavenly Father, can you please tell me/show me/let me sense one lie that I have believed from Satan about my health and the truth that you say about my health? (Write down what He shows you.)

3. Dear heavenly Father, can you please show me/tell me/let me sense one thing that you are doing in my children or my loved ones' lives now (name them)? (Write down what He shows you.)

SUMMARY

God is such an intimate God. He is interested in anything and everything that concerns your life. He is interested in your concerns about your health, fears, finances, the salvation of loved ones, children, career, life partner, ministry and the salvation of your loved ones. You can ask Him questions about your life and He can also ask you questions about your relationship with Him.

We can't possibly experience many of the promises of the Scripture unless we know God and hear Him speaking to us.

—Peter Lord, Hearing God

6

HOW DOES GOD SPEAK TO YOU?

Someone once commented, "When we pray to God, we call it praying. When God speaks back, we think that we are crazy." Your friends may even think you were out of your mind if you were to mention that you can hear God's voice. We have heard many stories of people who are persecuted because they claim they can hear God's voice. An example is Joan of Arc, a French peasant girl, who claimed that she heard divine voices telling her to fight against the English invaders; she was called a witch and eventually, was burned at the stake for heresy.

Just remember, the enemy will always try to counterfeit the genuine. In the Garden of Eden, Adam and Eve could hear God's voice even after they sinned. The most important thing is for you to learn how to discern the voices you have heard. Of course, if you hear a voice telling you to harm someone, you can be sure it is not God's voice because God will never ask you to do something that is contrary to His character or contradicts the Bible.

When I read Sandy Warner's book *101 Ways God Speaks*, I was intrigued as I could only count a maximum of ten ways—but again, I wouldn't limit God's ways to 101. Our God is infinitely creative, and He has many more ways than we can ever think of! If you are a parent with a number of children, it is very unlikely that you will use the same method to speak to each of your children, and even with each child, you may apply different methods depending on the particular situation, which again varies from one situation to another. As each child is different, you need to communicate at the appropriate level, taking into consideration, for example, the child's age, intellectual ability, and other developmental skills.

Braille was invented by Louis Braille and this helped blind people to read and write quickly and efficiently. This system, therefore, helps to bridge the gap in communication between the sighted and the blind. Sign language was invented because the deaf and mute needed a way to communicate with each other. If humans can use so many ways to communicate with each other, how much more will your Creator come up with infinite methods to communicate with you? He can use anything and anyone to communicate with you, though the main way He does this is through His written word.

Have you ever spoken to someone with the gift of gab and felt tempted to step out to see if they even noticed that you had stepped away? Were you ever with someone who answered with grunts or a one-syllable word? One-sided conversation makes you feel unappreciated and uncomfortable. A good conversation is likened to a tennis match with a back-and-forth exchange. As much as God wants you to talk to Him (most of the time you do this through your one-sided prayers), He also longs for you to listen to what He has to say.

Communication with God is never meant to be boring. There is nothing worse than a predictable God, where we know exactly what He will say each time. When your earthly parent speaks to you the same way on the same topic each time, don't you have the tendency to "switch off?" When we tell our son something that we've told him before, he says, "I know already. You've told me that before. You are repeating something that I've already heard and know." I feel our heavenly Father will get the same response from us if He keeps on telling us the same thing in the same way. Many people have been taught that God only communicates with them through the Bible. They are missing out so much on the dynamics of having other exciting adventures of communicating with God. Nothing can stop Him when He wants to speak to you, and He loves you too much to just leave you alone. He is in this love relationship with you to woo you so that you can know Him better. From God's perspective, the most important reason for hearing His voice is not just so that you will know the right things to do, but so you will know *Him*, your source of guidance in your life.

Jamie Galloway in his book, *Hearing God's Voice* wrote how uniquely God speaks to each one:

> *He never relates to two people in the same way because we are each designed differently. I like to think of it this way—some visual people are built like a HD TV, and they receive visions, dreams, and running pictures. Others are more audible, similar to an AM/FM radio; they receive messages or songs. You may not fit into either category. We serve a God who is so creative and multi-faceted.*

God speaks through the written word, like when you read the Bible, you hear God's voice, like a still small voice speaking into your heart when you begin to understand His words. God may speak to you in a gentle whisper like a lover showing His love and revealing His secrets. At times, He comes to minister to you, to comfort and encourage you, in a soft, gentle voice. At various times, God chooses to speak in audible words, and He may speak to you when you least expect it. God the Creator knows each of us so intimately; He knows the most effective way to get our attention and to accomplish His purposes.

God definitely speaks to nature and animals. There are many instances when God compares His people with the animals of the earth. In Jeremiah 8:7, God spoke of the stork who knows their appointed time; about the dove, the swift and the thrush which knows their migratory seasons. This is to show the people of Israel that they are ignorant of the requirements of the Lord. In Proverbs 6: 6-8, God uses the ant to teach the sluggard to be wise and to prepare for winter. In Luke 12:4

and Matthew 6:26, Jesus pointed to the ravens and other birds of the air in order to show to us that we are valuable to God and that He will provide for our needs as He does for the animals that He created.

Below are some of the more common ways that God has been known to communicate with His creation. However, the list is *not* exhaustive. One thing you need to realize is if you think that God only communicates with us through His Word, then all Satan needs to do is to stop you from reading His Word and then you will lose this communication channel. Are you not glad that God has infinite ways of communicating with you?

1. The different modes of communication God used in the Old Testament time:

- Angels (Genesis. 16:7; Exodus 14:19; Judges 6:11-22)
- Pillar of cloud by day (Exodus 14:19; Numbers 12:5)
- The judgment of the Urim & Thummim (Exodus 28:30; 1 Samuel 28:5-15; Numbers 27:21)
- The midst of darkness & blazing fire at Sinai (Deuteronomy 5:23,24,31)
- A gentle whisper; still, small voice (1 Kings 19:11-13)
- Using signs and fleeces (Genesis 9:12-15; Exodus 8:20-25; Joshua 10:12-14; Judges 6:37-40; Jeremiah 32:6-8)
- The prophetic words that were given to prophets (all the prophetic books in the Bible)
- External audible voice (I Samuel 3:1-21)
- Nature—In the thunder, hailstones, coals of fire, lightning, tornado and the heavens (Psalm 18:7-13; 19:1-6)
- Dreams & Visions (Genesis 15:1,12; 28:10,12; Numbers 12:6; 1 Samuel 3:15; 28:6,15; 1 Kings 3:5-15; Judges 7:13; Jeremiah 1:11-19; Daniel 1:17; 10:7)

2. The different modes of communication God used in the New Testament time and still uses today.

With the indwelling of Christ and the Holy Spirit in us, we can expect God to speak to us in myriads of new and exciting ways. We cannot limit how God may speak to us or else we will miss Him. The Bible documents some ways that God speaks to us in the New Testament and today:

- God's Son, Jesus Christ (Hebrews 1-4; John 1:1-4; Colossians 1:15-16)
- Signs (Luke 1:19-20)
- Words, teachings, the life of Jesus Christ (image of the invisible God) (Colossians 1:15-16)
- Healing and miraculous acts (Matthew 5:23-25; 10:1,8; Acts 4:30-33; 13:11; 16:16-18)
- Angels (Matthew 1:20; Luke 1:26; 2:9-14; Acts 12:7-15, 23; Hebrews 1:14, 13:2)
- Dreams and visions (Acts 2:17)
- Audible voice (Acts 22:6-16; 26:13-16)
- Prophecy (Luke 1:67; 2:25-35; Acts 2:17-18; 21:11; Revelation 19:10; 1 Corinthians 14:1-3; 13:9; 1 Timothy 1:18; 1 Thessalonians 5:19-22)
- Prophets (Luke 2:36-38; 1:13-17)
- Open and closed doors (Acts 16:6-7, 11-40; Acts 14:27; 1 Corinthians 16:5-9)
- Drawing lots and prayer (Acts 1:24-26)
- Circumstances; divine interruptions (Acts 22:6-16)
- Teachers, evangelists, pastors, apostles, prophets (Ephesians 4:11-12; Romans 10:14-15; 1 Thessalonians 5:12)
- The witness of the Holy Spirit in our spirit (Matthew 10:20; Romans 8:14,16; 2 Corinthians 3:3; Galatians 5:18; Ephesians 1:18; Hebrews 8:10)
- Gifts of the Holy Spirit (1 Corinthians 12:4-11, 14:1; Romans 1:11-12)
- The human heart (2 Corinthians 3:3; Hebrews 8:10) i.e. promptings, intuition, impressions in the heart
- The Church (Matthew 18:17; Hebrews 13:7; 1 Thessalonians 5:12-13)
- Other people (Hebrews 3:13; Matthew 18:19-20; 2 Corinthians 13:1; Romans 10:14; Proverbs 11:14; 15:22)

- Peace in the heart (John 14:27; Colossians 3:15; Philippians 4:7)
- Spiritual thoughts in the mind (2 Corinthians 3:3, Hebrews 8:10)
- Eyes of the heart (Ephesians 1:17)

The list is not exhaustive, but it will give you an idea of how creative God is in communicating with you. The Bible, which is the written Word, is primarily God's voice—and is fundamental for Christian living (see Psalm 119:105; 2 Timothy 3:16). We need to remind ourselves that God's Word is never outdated—whatever God has spoken in the past from the Old and New Testament times is applicable in the present day. His words are powerful and living and continue to move and speak throughout His creation.

Your heavenly Father speaks to you on your present level while always spurring you to move on, to grow, and to mature so that you can reach higher levels. You, therefore, graduate from "baby talk" to mature sons and daughters of God communicating with Him from a place of intimacy. You must develop your spiritual ears and give God the respect He deserves by listening to His voice and doing what He says. If you motivate yourself to pray, listen and obey, your life will become a great adventure.

How do you know when God is speaking to you? (1 Sam 3:1-10; John 10:3-5)

God the Creator wants to have fellowship with you—it's His desire to commune with you and He wants to hear from you all the time. By spending time in fellowship through prayers, quiet times and Bible reading, you will learn to recognize His voice when you listen to Him.

What does God's voice sound like?

When bank tellers are trained to recognize counterfeit money, they are given genuine money and asked to familiarize themselves with it. That way, when a counterfeit bill shows up, they are quick to recognize it.

This principle also applies when you are learning to hear God's voice. How can you be sure it's God's voice that you've heard? You can recognize His voice by familiarizing yourself with what He has already said in His Word (the Bible). When God speaks to you, whether audibly or in a still, small voice, He will say things that are in complete agreement with His Word and His character as portrayed in His Word.

God communicates from His Spirit to your spirit; His voice is very similar to your thoughts. His voice is never violent; He never contradicts the Scripture or tells you to do anything contrary to His Word. If I were to ask you to describe the character of God, you would come up with words like kind, loving, patient, full of grace, non-judgmental, merciful, faithful, and forgiving. These are all the marvelous attributes of God! When you hear His voice, you will know it's God because it will be in line with His character—instead of feeling agitated or afraid, you will find a comforting sense of peace over you.

Samuel was a young boy when he first heard God's voice and he did not recognize it until Eli, the chief priest instructed him (1 Samuel 3:1-2). Gideon witnessed God appearing before him, but still doubted what he had seen and heard, so he asked God for three signs as confirmation (Judges 6:17-22, 36-40). We have a distinct advantage over Samuel and Gideon in hearing God's voice as we have the complete Scripture from God to read and meditate upon. 2 Timothy 3:16-17 says, *"All Scripture is God-breathed and is useful for teaching, rebuking, correcting and training in righteousness, so that the man of God may be equipped for every good work."* Do you have a question about a decision that requires you to hear the voice of God? Study the Bible and see what it says. God never directs you in anything that is against what He has taught or promised in His Word.

WHAT ARE the characteristics of God's voice?

How do you discern God's voice? It depends on how well you know God's character and your relationship with Him. When you diligently seek Him, you will find Him. You can ask for wisdom in discerning His voice, and you can study God's Word in order to hear His voice.

Here are the basic characteristics of God's voice:

- Sounds very similar to your own thoughts
- May "hear" Him through pictures or images or through senses and impressions
- Is a voice of patience because He is never in a hurry
- Leads you but does not "drive" you
- Speaks with gentle leadings (1 Kings 19:11-13)
- Brings the sense that everything is under His control (Psalm 37:4)
- Gives clear-cut, specific directions (Acts 9:10-12)
- Convicts you of specific sin (John 16:8)
- Will not contradict the Scripture (John 14:6)
- Builds faith and brings peace, joy, righteousness, and love in your life (Philippians 4:7)
- Will encourage, edify, or comfort you (Ephesians 4:12)
- Instructs and corrects you in righteousness and causes you to profit in Christ (2 Timothy 3:16)
- Brings His Word to your remembrance (John 14:26)
- Guides you into all truth (John 16:13)
- This leads you to salvation (Romans 10:9-10, 2 Timothy 3:15)
- Assures you of His love towards you (1 John 3:1, Jeremiah 31:3)
- Increases your faith (Romans 10:17)
- It causes you to triumph in life through Christ (2 Corinthians 2:14)

Mark Virkler explained it this way in his book, *Hearing God through Biblical Meditation*:

> *When God speaks to you, it may be through 'spontaneous' thoughts. 'Spontaneous' means that the thoughts seem to just appear in your hearts. They are not just something that you were already thinking about. When God speaks to you, you feel His peace or faith or conviction or excitement. He does this by putting thought, a word, an idea, a feeling, an impression or a vision in your heart.*

God's voice is based on Biblical truths. His Word is powerful and living. When God speaks, you can sense His love, compassion, grace, and mercy. God's voice is comforting, encouraging, enlightening and reassuring. Of course, it is important to check every thought or feeling, prompting or a vision, against the Word of the Bible so as to check whether or not it agrees with His written Word and His character.

In his book, *Perfecting the Prophetic,* Les Crause made this statement:

> *If you study the Scriptures, you will eventually begin to get an idea of how God thinks. Then when somebody gives a prophetic word, you can immediately judge that word by saying, 'Okay, that lines up with the way God thinks. It lines up with the way He normally speaks,' or you could say, 'I have never heard God speak that way before. This just doesn't sound right. It doesn't sound like the God I know.'*

In Steve & Evy Klassen's book, *Your Ears will Hear—A Journal for Listening to God,* they give this advice about how they know that God is speaking to them:

In tuning in to my inner voice I didn't audibly hear 'voices,' rather I just monitored the random unconnected images, notions, and thoughts that floated through my head. Becoming aware of them I'd check them out using the following criteria. It's by no means a complete list, but for me, it was an essential tool for discernment. I considered my random unconnected thoughts from God if they were: peaceful, consistent, loving, patient, uplifting, instructive, comforting, clear, kind, welcoming of scrutiny, seldom needing to be responded to in a hurry.

What does Satan's voice sound like?

Satan's voice will also sound like thoughts in your mind and that is why many people get side-tracked when they try to hear God's voice. There is a lot of fear among Christians that they will hear Satan's voice instead of God's voice when they are seeking God's direction. Because of this fear, some pastors have discouraged their congregation from seeking to hear God's voice and have directed them to the Bible if they want any answers for their lives. These pastors have failed to differentiate between the *Logos* (written word of God) and the *Rhema* (spoken word of God).

If I ask you this question, "Who do you perceive as more powerful-God or Satan?" I'm sure I know what answer you'll give. Your answer will allay the fear of hearing Satan's voice when you have specifically asked God to let you hear His voice. Once you realize and believe that God is more powerful than Satan, then you will know that God can stop Satan from interfering with your communication with Him. You will be able to discern who is speaking to you once you learn what the voices of God and Satan sound like. The voices of God and Satan are completely different. This includes what is said, how it's said, and the impact that it has on you. The easiest way for you to get better at discerning the difference between God's voice and Satan's is to get to know Jesus because Jesus will reveal the Father to you.

Satan will always try to infiltrate your thoughts. I am sure that you have watched cartoons in which there's one character with a halo and another character with horns sitting on someone's shoulders and whispering to them to do something either good or bad. This represents the good and the evil thoughts speaking to you all the time. The most important question is: Who will you listen to? Isn't it scary when people who've done horrific killings in many countries today claim that it was God who instructed them to do the killing? You might have read on the news that there are also people who've killed their loved ones and then said, "God told me to do this because they were evil, and they deserved to die." If you know the character of God and His voice, you know He will never ask you to do something contrary to what the Scripture says. Once you recognize God's voice, you will be able to know when it is Satan speaking to you.

Satan is the enemy, he is a deceiver and an accuser. He is always roaming around, looking to cause you pain, and provoking you to sin and trying so hard to separate you from God. You have to stand firm on God's Word. Psalm 91 talks of God's protection over you. The enemy cannot harm you and you have been given power over the devil to trample him down, so you should be free from fear.

What are the characteristics of Satan's voice?

From the Bible, we can learn of the characteristics of Satan's voice as revealed in the following passages:

- May quote Scriptures that are half-truths or out of context (Luke 4:10-11)
- Will try to deceive you (Revelation 20:7-8)
- Will try to imitate God's voice as he can transform himself to appear as an angel of light (2 Corinthians 11:14)
- Will cause you to doubt God's Word (Hebrews 3:12)
- Can speak through the mouth of someone else (e.g. Peter in Mark 8:33)
- It causes you to despair by telling you: "You have missed it" or "All is lost"
- It causes you to become bitter (Colossians 3:19)
- It brings fear to you (Mark 4:40)
- It causes you to feel hopelessness (Job 7:1-15)
- It causes you to rationalize sin (Isaiah 5:20)
- It makes you feel dismayed (Joshua 1:9)
- It blinds your mind (2 Corinthians 4:4)
- It brings anxiety, despair, confusion, and fear to you
- It will hastily pressure you into situations, i.e. to push you to do something now and therefore, does not allow you to think or seek Godly counsel first
- It brings guilt and condemnation and makes you feel that God is angry or not pleased with you.

As you can see, Satan's voice is demanding, critical and condemning, resulting in guilt and confusion. Satan seeks to destroy your relationship with your heavenly Father, by misrepresenting God's goodness, and inciting you against your fellow beings—he is the accuser of brethren (Revelation 12:10).

Satan's favorite line of attack is to question you on your sonship and righteous standing with God. For example, he will ask you questions such as:

- Are you sure that God loves you?
- Are you sure that He will forgive you or has forgiven you for what you have done?
- Are you sure that He will hear you when you pray when you have not lived a holy life?

In Luke 3:21-22, after John baptized Jesus, God said to Jesus, *"You are my beloved Son, in whom I am well pleased."* God said this before Jesus performed any miracles. God's approval had *nothing* to do with Jesus' performance throughout His ministry. Satan, when tempting Jesus in the wilderness kept on asking Jesus, "If you are the son of God..." (Luke 4:3,9) even though Jesus had already received affirmation from God that He is God's beloved son. Yet Satan tried to sway Him and cause doubts about this truth. How much more will he try to get you to doubt that you are the son/daughter of the heavenly Father with whom He is well pleased? You need not earn His approval through your own efforts. He already approves of you and He loves you unconditionally.

What do you do if you think that you are hearing Satan's voice?

In Luke 4:1-13, we read how Satan tempted Jesus to turn against His heavenly Father—and failed! Satan tried to control Jesus by questioning His divine Sonship—"If you are the Son of God..." Satan quoted half-truths from the Scripture, but Jesus was able to rebuff the attacks by responding with the truth of God's Word.

When Satan whispers lies or tempts you to sin, be like Jesus who said, "This is what the Word of God says..."—you must replace the lies of Satan with truth from God's Word. This is the reason why it is so important to know God's Word, so that you will recognize Satan's wiles of half-truths and deception. When your thoughts bring fear, anxiety, and worries, you must remember to replace your thoughts with God's truth. You must learn to bring every thought that you have in captivity to the mind of Christ (2 Corinthians 10:5), then Satan's voice will have no place in your thoughts.

If you hear a thought that is forceful, you will know that this thought is definitely not from God. The Lord's voice is gentle, and He will lead us by the hand. He will not slap you on the face and force you to do something that you do not want to do. If He were forceful, He would have forced you to receive His salvation, but instead, He has given you the free choice to choose.

If you hear a voice that tells you, "You must do this now or you will be cursed," then you know that this is not the voice of the Lord but of Satan. Jesus never told his disciples, "You better go out now, two by two, or I will curse you." When you know the character of our Lord, you will be able to discern if what you have heard is from Him or not. If you hear a voice that tells you that God is angry with you because you did not give a prophetic word when prompted by the Holy Spirit and you felt guilt and fear, you can be sure that this is the voice of Satan. The voice of God will never bring fear or guilt or condemnation to you.

What does your own voice sound like?

Your own voice can either be critical, hard and condemning, or swing to the other side of the pendulum where you end up being too easy on yourself. If you are hard, critical, and condemning with yourself, you will most likely use this same yardstick with other people. However, if you are too easy on yourself, this will cause you to have a lack of spiritual discipline in your life and you will begin to live your life against God's word. Your own voice tends to start with "I," e.g. "I am not good enough," "I am useless," "I always fail," "I can never do this."

Many times, your own voice can come across as the voice of reasoning (Acts 2:6-8). The Lord has given you the ability to reason and to be able to rationally consider all options, advantages versus disadvantages, consequences, etc. You can always tell when you are listening to the voice of your own reasoning. This is because you will weigh the things you see and hear in the natural. You will also deliberate and think things through, then make your own decision. A word of caution here —if the decision or the potential outcome contradicts the written Word, or is contrary to God's character, then you must abandon the voice of your reasoning (Numbers 13:26-33).

Your own voice may also be the voice of your flesh (Galatians 5:16-21). You will know that you are being led by the voice of the flesh when you engage in adultery, witchcraft, hatred, strife, envy, wrath, etc. The voice of the flesh will never inspire you to do the will of God. What you need to do with the voice of the flesh is to bring it into subjection to God's Word (1 Corinthians 9:27).

Your own voice can be the voice of your conscience (Acts 24:16, Hebrews 10:22). Your conscience is the place where you recognize the difference between what is right and what is wrong. It is the place where you establish morals and values, or where you reject good morals and values. You can listen to your voice of conscience as long as you have a good conscience (1 Timothy 1:4), but when you have a weak conscience (1 Corinthians 8:7), a seared conscience (1 Timothy 4:2), or an evil conscience (Hebrews 10:22), then you should not yield to the voice of your conscience.

Your thoughts are analytical and cognitive. For example, when you wake up in the morning, the first thing you may do is to plan your day using your thoughts. You will make mental notes of appointments, work schedules or chores that you need to do around the house, meeting friends, cooking meals, etc. You live this way out of your reasoning process. These thoughts are limited by your own knowledge, wisdom, understanding, and abilities.

How can you discern God's voice from the voices of Satan and your own voice?

1. God speaks deep within your spirit, whereas Satan speaks to your soul or mind.
2. God's voice is gentle and persuasive, free from pressure, whereas Satan's voice is loud and demanding an immediate response.
3. God says, "This is what you ought to do," whereas Satan tends to scream to your thoughts and say, "This is what you *have* to do!"
4. God's voice imparts peace and stills the soul. It gives you the sense that everything is under control because *He* is in control. Satan's voice will tell you that everything is out of control and that you will lose everything because you have sinned, or that God does not love you anymore.
5. God's voice brings you the assurance that all will be well and that there is hope. Satan's voice brings thoughts of hopelessness, helplessness, or the "all is lost" feeling and also cause you to fear.
6. God's voice is always clear and distinct, giving you a clear direction on which way to go (Isaiah 30:21), for He is not the author of confusion (1 Corinthians 14:33). Satan's voice makes you worry, causes confusion, and leads to a loss of direction.
7. God's voice does not hurry you. Even if you lack direction or are uncertain about which way to go, you can wait. God does not mind waiting for His children to discern His will. Satan's voice will rush, push, and drive you to do something when you are not sure which direction you should take.
8. God's voice speaks to you when you are seeking and listening for Him. Satan breaks into your thoughts uninvited, making you angry, jealous, or fearful.
9. God's voice convicts you of specific sins. He leaves you in no doubt about what you need to confess and repent of (for example, He could say, "Yesterday, you spoke unkindly to this person and you should apologize to her.") Satan's voice speaks in generalities and justifies sin and causes you to feel guilt and condemnation.
10. God's voice brings encouragement, comfort, and reassurance

whereas Satan's voice brings discouragement, discomfort, and fear.

Mark Virkler, in his book, *Hearing God through Biblical Meditation* gave this advice:

> *Any words you receive that cause you to fear or doubt, bring you into confusion or anxiety, or stroke your ego (especially if you hear something that is 'just for you alone— no one else is worthy') must be immediately rebuked and rejected as lies of the enemy.*

How do you know if a revelation that you are receiving is really of the Lord and not one of your fancy ideas? If you are getting a thought that sounds logical and sensible and is based on your intuition, or what you already know and are thinking about—then you are most likely hearing your own voice. The voice of your mind will bring thoughts that you are already thinking about. When God tells you to do something or puts spontaneous thoughts in your mind, it will defy a common logic or understanding. It will be something that you have never thought about or considered before. Someone likened the thoughts that come to you from God as like a river flowing inside of you and bubbling to the surface. These thoughts seem to "light up" in your mind without it being forceful. God's ideas are fresh, new, exciting, and sometimes challenging, because He may ask you to do something outside of your comfort zone. You should also check your thoughts for any "motives," for example, ask yourself if this idea will encourage others or edify the church, or is this for your selfish ends or some sort of ego-trip? Surely then you will know where the "impure motives" come from. Reject them straight away! Don't worry, the Holy Spirit is always available to you to guide, counsel, comfort, and encourage you in this new adventure of learning to discern God's voice from other voices.

Stanley, Scott, Wood, and Brandon in their book, *The Voice of God,* wrote:

> *I put them down as coming from myself rather than the spiritual realms if they were in a logical processed outcome of things I'd learned or deduced; appealed to my ego; varied all the time depending on the information I'd received or would eventually make me look good in front of others.*

When you are unsure whether what you heard is from God, Satan, or your own voice, ask this question, "Would Jesus says this?" As you test the voice, remember the character of Jesus (compassionate, kind, gentle, forgiving, loving, faithful, etc.). Also, remember how Jesus spoke to those who were sick, demon-possessed or in sin, and you will be able to discern whether what you hear is from Him or not. The truth of the matter is that the more clearly you can hear God's voice, the more accountable He holds you to obey what He says to you (Luke 12:47-48). One person once said to me, "I have no problem hearing God's voice, but my problem is obeying what He shows/tells me to do." When you hear God's voice, you must commit to obey Him.

Prayer

Dear heavenly Father, please teach me how to discern Your voice when you are speaking to me. As I learn more about Your character, I know that I will be more confident in knowing when You speak to me. Help me to be able to discern the voice of Satan and my own voice. I want to only obey Your voice and the truths You said about me. In Jesus' name. Amen.

Activation exercises

1. You are at a crossroads regarding your job, finance, health, marriage or life partner. Ask God a question regarding any of the above. For example, "Dear heavenly Father, can you please show me/tell me/let me sense what I should do regarding my current job situation. Write down all the thoughts that come to your mind after you have asked the questions. Do not try to differentiate the thoughts whether they are from God, Satan or your own voice. Once you finish writing all the thoughts, apply the following questions:

a. What is the thought saying to me? Does it sound like what God would say?

b. Does the thought bring me fear, condemnation or confusion or does it bring me peace? Which thoughts sound like what God would say to me?

c. Does the thought come like a river flowing through me and bubble to the surface? If so, how did it make me feel? Do I think that the thought is from God?

d. Does the thought sound like a logical and sensible thing for me to do? Do I think that the thought is from God, Satan, or from me based on what I have learned?

2. You have been approached by someone who wants to sell you a business. The person that is selling the business tells you that you need to make a decision soon or else he will sell to someone else. You are not sure whether you should buy the business or not, you feel "rushed" to make a decision, but at the same time, you do not want to lose out to

someone else. Making use of what you have learned about the various voices that you could hear, how would you go about finding out whether the business is something God wants you to buy? Write down how God's voice, your voice, and Satan's voice would sound. Based on the knowledge and understanding that you have just learned and at the same time asking the Holy Spirit to lead you, what decision would you make?

SUMMARY

It is important for you to learn to discern God's voice from other voices which you may hear. God's voice will never contradict His character and His Word. His voice brings peace, joy, love, and grace. Thoughts from God are as if a river is flowing inside of you and bubbling to the surface. Satan's voice brings condemnation, fear, and guilt. If you hear something that is logical and seems like a sensible thing to do, it is most probably your own voice. When you are not sure which voice you are hearing, you can ask, "Would Jesus/God say this?"

When God speaks to you, he is not writing a new book of Scripture; rather, He is applying to your life what He has already said in his Word.

—Henry T. Blackaby, *Hearing God's Voice*

7

HOW DOES GOD USE YOUR FIVE SPIRITUAL SENSES TO SPEAK TO YOU?

The most common way that God speaks to you is through His Word, but many times He uses your five spiritual senses to speak to you. This is because the Bible is confined and limited by the necessities of ink and paper. We know that the Word of God is alive and active. Many people wrongly think that a silent God suddenly spoke through inspiring the holy men and prophets to write, and after the book was written, He lapsed into silence forever. When you read the Bible, you learn of God's wisdom, His ways, and His character as the written Word of God, which is the *"Logos."* As you begin to meditate on the written Word, the Holy Spirit may quicken the Word within you, specifically for you and for that specific situation. When the quickened written Word speaks to you personally, it becomes the *"Rhema"* word from God.

God speaks to you through your five spiritual senses

Just as you have five physical senses of sight, hearing, smell, taste, and touch, you also have five spiritual senses that God uses as modes to communicate with you. These are visual (seeing), auditory (hearing), and perceptive (touch, smell, and taste) modes. Many Christians do not believe they have any spiritual senses. However, you can hear some Christians relating the times when Satan has tempted them. They couldn't have heard Satan's voice if they didn't have any spiritual senses. Somehow, many people have more faith that the devil can speak to them than that God can speak to them. It is clear throughout the Bible that we have spiritual eyes and ears. In Ezekiel 12:2, God said to Ezekiel, *"Son of man, you live in the midst of the rebellious house who have eyes to see but do not see, ears to hear but do not hear; for they are a rebellious house."*

God uses your five spiritual senses to communicate with you in such a way that the Scriptures come to life. When you read the Bible silently, you are only using your eyes to read, your mouth to verbalize, and your ears to hear. The physical process of reading aloud translates from using the natural senses to the spiritual and shows the activation of three spiritual senses. Everyone has at least one spiritual sense that God uses to communicate with them. Often, you receive messages from God where He uses a combination of the different spiritual senses. For example, you may hear a trumpet blare and at the same time, you see a picture of the trumpet in your mind. God can use any number of spiritual senses to speak to you so you should remain open to whichever senses God chooses to communicate with you. You may even discover new and exciting experiences at various seasons when the different senses are deployed. Therefore, you should not be surprised when God suddenly switches to using a different spiritual sense to communicate with you.

How does God use the five spiritual senses to communicate with you?

1. Through the spiritual sense of sight

Many times, Biblical truths of the Bible are presented through story, vision, symbol, and narrative. Some Biblical experts suggest that 70% of the Bible is presented as images. When you look at how God communicated with His prophets, He often uses image-based visions.

There are many examples of God communicating with the various prophets and ordinary people using the visual mode.

- Isaiah reported his visionary experiences this way: "The word which Isaiah the son of Amos saw" (Isaiah 2:1, 13:1).
- Jeremiah described what he "saw" as the word of the Lord (Jeremiah 1:11, 13; 24:3).
- Micah said, "The word of the Lord which came to Micah… which he saw" (Micah 1:1).
- Zechariah says that the "Word of the Lord" came to him and during the night, he had a vision (Zechariah 1:7-8).
- Amos says, "The Lord God showed me" (Amos 7:1, 4, 7; 8:1).

Ezekiel tells us that the visions of God that he saw are "the Word of the Lord" (Ezekiel 1:3).

In the New Testament, God continues to speak to His children using the visual mode. Many times, this is through dreams and visions. Various examples are given below:

- The angel appears before Zechariah (Luke 1:11-22).
- God spoke to Ananias in a vision (Acts 9:10).
- God spoke to Cornelius in a vision through an angel (Acts 10:3).

Paul has a vision of a man of Macedonia (Acts 16:9).

Jerame Nelson in his book, *Activating Your Spiritual Senses,* gave this advice:

> *One of the greatest things we can do to boost our spiritual sight is to read the Word. The Word of God will bring an impartation or framework to you, so you can see. If you want to see heaven, then start reading about heaven in the Bible. Read Revelation chapter four and five over and over again and, ask God to open your sense of sight and to release to you the Spirit of Wisdom and Revelation and watch what happens.*

Though all of us have the spiritual sense of sight as part of our DNA, each of us views life in our own individual way. This can be influenced by our upbringing, education, culture, and life experiences. When God opens your spiritual sense of sight, it will draw you to grow in the ability to see life from God's eternal perspective. Visualizing from God's perspective will enable you to grow more like your heavenly Father in thought and character. It will also motivate you to work according to His plan and His purposes for your life. You need to use your spiritual eyes to see and not your physical eyes. In 2 Corinthians 4:18, we are encouraged to *"fix our eyes not on what is seen, but on what is unseen as what is seen is temporary but what is unseen is eternal."*

God can show you images/visions in color or in black and white, in the form of a still picture or a moving image like in a movie. For example, if I ask you to close your eyes and see your bedroom in your imagination, you should be able to see your bedroom as a single still picture. However, if I ask you to imagine driving your car from your home to work, you would most likely see various moving screens in your imagination. Another example would be if a friend was talking about a red fire truck, you could "see" the picture of that red fire truck in your mind. The Lord will project images within your mind. As your mind is being renewed, you will have "the mind of Christ." Your imagination will become "sanctified" and you can more easily discern if the images are from the Lord or not. You can experience seeing such visions either when your eyes are shut or opened.

I have noticed that God initially tends to use the visual mode to speak to people who watch a lot of television or use a lot of computers, as this is a sure way to grab their attention. A young man who attended one of my training courses on hearing God's voice discovered that God was speaking to him in the form of a Powerpoint presentation. This means that God flashed one slide in his mind and then another slide after that. This was because he had used a lot of PowerPoint presentations in his studies. God speaks to another lady whom I know by showing her a word in a big font, for example, FAITH. The word then moves around her and surrounds her so she can't miss what God is trying to say to her.

God can show you a broad-based picture that zooms in on a specific detail. He may also show you a picture superimposed over an actual scene as you are viewing in the natural. The image that you see may quickly flash before your "mind's eye," then fade away or become still, after which you are left with a memory of the picture.

As they say, "A picture paints a thousand words"—how true indeed! A picture certainly conveys many details and much information all at once. If you don't understand what you see, you can always ask God to show you the picture again so that you can get more details. He will then clarify whatever questions you may have.

God showed Amos various visions (Amos 7:1, 4, 8:1, 9:1). He even interacted with Amos. God asked Amos, "What do you see, Amos?" When Amos pleaded with God not to destroy Israel, God relented. As Amos was obedient to what God asked him to do, he began to have a better understanding of the plan and the purpose God had for the nation of Israel. Apostle John received end-time revelation when he was in the spirit on the island of Patmos (Revelation 1:9-12). He heard a loud voice like a trumpet telling him to write what he saw. He turned around to see who was speaking to him and he saw Jesus standing by the lamp stands.

God created you in His likeness (Genesis 1:27) and since God has a mind, so do you. The mind is where your thoughts, ideas, and decisions are formed. God wants you to put on the mind of Christ and to set your mind on what is above (Colossians 3:2) and to grow in your relationship with Him.

Paul prayed that *"the eyes of your heart may be enlightened so that you will know what is the hope of His calling, what are the riches of the glory of His inheritance in the saints"* (Ephesians 1:18). Where are your spiritual eyes within you? Your spiritual eyes operate within the faculty where images are formed, and this is what we commonly call "imagination." "Imagination" means "image producing." Imagination happens when pictures are created in your mind. Your imagination is created by God so that you can communicate with the unseen realm. Every person has this faculty. Whether you realize it or not, you use your imagination every day. God's will is made known to you because the imagination is the place where He often speaks to you through dreams and visions. Your imagination is a powerful path to prophetic revelation, and it is one of the avenues that God uses to reveal His will to you.

However, this faculty has been strongly condemned by some religious groups because of its potential to become corrupted and used immorally. Your imagination may have been bombarded by the world and clouded with unholy images and by your experiences. Because of these thoughts, you are often afraid to use or exercise your imagination. You may shut down your imagination and this will hinder your ability to hear God correctly.

For most of us, our imagination is a strategic battleground within us. You can either yield your imagination to the power of darkness or to Jesus Christ; it has the potential for either good or bad. It can create or be subject to evil images or godly images, depending on to whom you surrender and dedicate this important visual faculty of your mind. If you dedicate and surrender to the Holy Spirit, then God can use that faculty to bring visual revelation to you. When you surrender your imaginations daily to the Lord, renewing your mind with the truth of God and with regular practice, you will begin to strengthen this visual faculty so that it is yielded to the Lord only. The Lord can then initiate revelations, visions, and other prophetic experiences in your encounters with God.

God can use your imagination to communicate His specific plans and definite purposes in your life. Thoughts that are from God are always encouraging and build up your faith. In the Bible, we read that God is always thinking about us. It is because of our fallen sin nature that thoughts of ourselves do not align with God's thoughts of us. If you let God fill your thoughts with His truths, you will find much encouragement in your Christian journey.

In Keith A. Paul's book, *Increasing the Seer Anointing*, he made the following observations:

> *Almost without exception, every person has the ability to*

formulate images of things familiar. For instance, if you were to describe in detail a favorite childhood memory, playground, picnic, event, family setting or place, your memory would likely access the visual, emotional and verbal information stored in your memory banks. The emotional and verbal information is also important. It is there in the visual mode that the Holy Spirit releases images or visions. These visions may be of past events at first. In fact, the Holy Spirit will usually begin there because those are familiar scenes that you are sure of because you lived them. The Holy Spirit will then take you into a replay of events that may have occurred recently or today. He reviews them with us. Notice the word review. This is actually what happens. The Holy Spirit will then begin to give us images of random events that possibly could happen tomorrow as we project our thoughts toward some specific task. He will train us in this if we listen and pay attention.

Do you know that you can use someone else's vision to activate your own experience in His presence? Let's say you don't use much of your visual faculty throughout the day and the only thing that you look at are words, and maybe a few images here and there. You may even be so used to your surroundings that you don't even "see" anymore. Then later, you meet someone who shares what God has shown them in a picture about peace (for example). If that picture resonates with you and you can relate to the picture, you can "borrow" this person's picture and store it in your memory bank as a picture of peace. The Holy Spirit may then start with this stored picture and then lead you into an application that is more personalized later on. It is likened to "priming" your visual faculty to get it going so that you are ready to get more pictures from the Lord for yourself.

Kenneth MacDonald in his book, *Prophetic Seminar Handbook* shared the following example about imagination from his conversation with the late Bob Jones:

 Bob says, 'I will tell you that all prophecy begins in your imagination.' Bob said to me, 'Look at this and tell me what you

see.' I looked where he was pointing and saw a clear glass of ice water, with a round, green slice of lime floating on the top. Bob said, 'Close your eyes and tell me what you see.' I closed my eyes and said, 'Well, I see the glass of ice water with the green slice of lime floating in it.' He said, 'That's right. Your mind is like a television set, and the Lord can send you pictures or ideas, and moving pictures just like you are watching a movie all the time.'

How do you activate your "seeing" faculty?

Practically, how does this work? You may get frustrated when someone who "sees" in the spiritual realm says that you are able to see but doesn't tell you how. I used to feel the same frustration as well. When I was under the prophetic mentorship with Prophet Russell Walden from Father's Heart Ministry, I was so glad he shared freely the "how." I am so grateful I have learned so much from him and he has freely given his interns permission to use his teaching material—which I will share with you as you go further.

Keith A. Paul in his book, *Prophetic Seer Anointing*, gave the following advice:

> *We can see better with our eyes closed. When we position ourselves in the receptive mode, we will first of all shut out the natural distractions that come through the natural eyes. It is there in our spirit that we gaze through the inner eyes of the spirit and receive visions and go into trances.*

Let me show you step-by-step how to experience "seeing" for yourself. You will begin to realize that all of us can "see" and are already "seeing."

I want you to close your eyes and picture the front of your house. What do you see in your thoughts/mind? If you have beautiful flowers at the front of your house, you will most likely "see" the flowers in your mind. If weeds are at the front of your house, then you will "see" weeds. Now close your eyes and picture your car. Can you see the color of your car in your mind? What color is the seat cover? What's just taken place is that you "saw" a mental picture in your mind. When the image or picture is projected into your mind, you didn't see it outwardly with your physical eyes, what you see is on the inside—this is what we call the "mind's eye." What you saw was a "still" picture.

What is a "moving" picture? When you see a vision, it may be a series of moving pictures like what you see when watching TV or a movie on the big screen. Sometimes you may even feel like you are an outside observer, looking at your own situation.

Let's see how this works. Close your eye and think of a black dog. Now think of a yellow canary. Now picture the black dog chasing the yellow canary. This is how you see in the spiritual realm when God shows you a vision. Vision seems to be like a very big spiritual word when it is just describing a moving picture that changes to the next scene (like when you are watching TV or a movie). You do not need to have super-vision, where you leave your body or see people's private lives. God can show you the kind of vision where you see a picture in the spirit and God uses it to show you what He wants to say. If you do not understand the picture that God has shown you, you can ask Him to explain it to you. Remember that God delights to dialogue with you and that showing you the picture is just an invitation to you to have an extended dialogue with Him.

One way that you can develop your spiritual sight's muscles is to read the Bible and ask God to show you a picture of what you have just read. For example, when you read Psalm 23:1-2, ask the Holy Spirit to show you a picture/vision of Jesus as the Shepherd, the green pastures, and the quiet waters. When you read Psalm 91:4, you can also ask the Holy Spirit to show you a picture of the Lord covering you with His feathers and then asking Him to let you sense how you feel when you are under His wings. You can also ask the Holy Spirit to show you a picture of the refuge.

2. Through the spiritual sense of hearing

Another method God uses to communicate with you is through hearing Him. The Lord *"told Samuel in his ear before Saul came"* (1 Samuel 9:15-17). Those in the upper room "heard" the sound of a mighty rushing wind (Acts 2:2). John heard behind him a loud voice like the sound of a trumpet (Revelations 1:10). God caused their spiritual sense of hearing to be opened on that day.

In Mark 4:9, we read that Jesus was teaching a large group of people using parables. When He had finished speaking, He said to them, *"He who has ears to hear, let him hear."* The natural hearing takes place when you listen, but spiritual listening is the ability to listen deeply and to hear with your spiritual ears. Adam and Eve heard the Lord God walking in the garden in the cool of the day. When the Lord called Adam and said to him, "Where are you?" Adam replied that he'd *heard* God's voice in the garden, but he hid because he was afraid due to his nakedness (Genesis 3: 8-10). Though sin broke their fellowship with God, He still desired to commune with Adam and Eve, just as He desires to commune with you.

How do you activate the spiritual sense of hearing?

Let me show you step-by-step how this works. I want you to think about your favorite song or the "Happy Birthday" song. Hear it play in your head. Did you hear the song in your thoughts? Think of your first name and last name silently to yourself. Did you hear your name as you thought of it? That was the voice of your own thought. Your physical ears were not engaged, but you "heard" something. You heard because most of the "hearing" takes place in your thought, not in your ears. This is how you hear God's still, small voice. The Lord speaks, and you hear something on the inside. It works very much in the same way as seeing, except you hear the voice. You hear something on the inside, like intensely focused and flowing/spontaneous thoughts.

When God bypasses your physical ears and drops words and sentences into your mind, it sounds the same as the voice of your own thought. God can speak to you by recalling something to your memory or bringing Scripture or songs back into your mind by you "hearing" it. God uses words and sentences and most of the time the voice is seldom audible. You don't usually hear Him with your physical ears but hear Him in your thoughts.

Hearing from God is easier to understand than when God shows you a picture because you do not need to interpret what you have heard. However, the disadvantage is that since what you have heard sounds so much like your own thoughts, you may find it difficult to discern whether it is the Lord's voice or your own voice. To safeguard yourself, you must always filter what you hear using the Scriptures. If you did not hear Him clearly the first time, you can ask Him to clarify and confirm the message to you. Someone gave this valuable advice to me: *"If it's exactly what you wanted to hear, it's probably your own voice you're hearing. But if it's challenging, re-orienting, and sounds impossible to be done, then it is most probably God."* If the voice you hear is telling you to do something to help, to encourage someone, or to call someone, then you know definitely it is not from the enemy. What you heard could not be your voice, as you hadn't thought about it, and it's also out of your comfort zone. By the process of elimination, you can easily discern God's voice from the enemy or your own voice.

3. Through the spiritual sense of smell

The spiritual sense of smell is not as common as seeing or hearing, but God does use this to communicate with you as well. The smell is the one sense which you may sometimes consider as unimportant. For example, when you catch a cold or have hay fever, you sometimes lose your sense of smell. Unlike your other senses, you don't panic about this loss of smell as you know that it will soon return. Smell clings to you (either good or bad smells). You can't always see what you smell. A smell can be carried along by the air currents and drift far from its source. Therefore, smell/odor can be detected long after the source has stopped emitting the odor. The sense of smell is a more intimate sense than most other senses because what you smell tends to almost become a part of you (imagine freshly baked bread or the smell of barbecuing meat). In detecting a smell, you absorb the essence of it. This could be a bad smell, as in when you walk past a rubbish dump or a good smell when you smell the aroma of frying bacon and eggs or the aroma of coffee when you wake up in the morning. Where food is concerned, you normally smell before you taste it and you reject any food that smells "off" no matter how delicious it looks.

When you think of the God of the Bible, you always picture Him "watching over you," but there is biblical evidence that God has a divine "olfactory sense." In Genesis 8:21, you read that following the flood, Noah came out of the ark and sacrificed burnt offerings on an altar. The Lord smelled the pleasing aroma and said that He would never again curse the ground because of humans, even though every inclination of the human heart is evil from childhood. He will never again destroy all living creatures. God was moved to mercy by the smell of the simple burnt offering of Noah.

In 2 Corinthians 2:14, Paul says that we are the fragrance of life to God and that we are the aroma of His Son, Jesus. The knowledge of Jesus is a fragrance that clings to you. You can smell the purity of Jesus. You can smell His presence. Holiness has a fragrance. The Word says that God smells our fragrance, and He spreads it, allowing the beautiful fragrance of the knowledge of His Son to permeate into the hearts of others. According to Revelation 5:8, our prayers are incense in golden bowls before God's throne. In Psalm 141:2, we read that "our prayer is like incense to God." Can you smell the fragrance of your prayer life as it rises up to God like incense?

The sense of smell can also be related to the discerning of spirits. Sometimes you may have the ability to smell the fragrance of the Lord (Psalm 45:8). Many people have testified to sensing the presence of the Lord accompanied by the smell of roses. However, sometimes you can also smell the enemy's presence (a foul smell, like rotten eggs or sour milk or Sulphur smell) when you enter a location or a house. If there is no logical, natural explanation for the unpleasant odor, it may be an indicator to you that an unclean spirit is present. Some people can smell a bad odor of cancer or death because Satan's kingdom stinks and odors can be attached to sickness and death.

Kenneth MacDonald, in his book, *Prophetic Seminar Handbook*, mentioned that he is able to discern a smell like that of a "wet dog" when he meets someone who is a homosexual because of the unclean spirit operating in that person. He can also smell "battery acid" in a person who is addicted to drugs and those who are addicted to alcohol have a "musty breath."

Once a friend and I visited a home which I had never been to before. When the owner of the house opened the door, I could distinctly smell something that was foul and obnoxious. I thought that maybe it was the smell of food from a different culture that I was not familiar with. Before we ended the visit, the owner of the house requested that we pray for her. When we started to pray, the person manifested, and I could distinctly smell the foul smell again. This time I realized that the foul smell was from an evil spirit. That was the first time that my spiritual smell was so heightened that I could smell the presence of a foul spirit.

Activation on the sense of smell

1. Imagine that you have just woken up and someone is cooking bacon. What does it smell like?

2. Imagine that someone has just baked a fresh loaf of bread. What does it smell like?

3. Imagine that you have just cracked a rotten egg on the frying pan. What does it smell like?

4. 2 Corinthians 2:15 reads, "We are the fragrance of Christ to God among those who are being saved and among those who are perishing." Ask God to let you smell His fragrance emitting from you. What do you think you smell like?

4. The spiritual sense of touch/feeling

God can speak to you through the sense of touch. Unlike some other senses, touch requires proximity. You can see, smell, or hear a person from a distance, but to touch someone or something, you need to be up close. Sometimes your eyes and ears can deceive you but when you are able to feel touch, it grounds you and makes you believe what you hear and see is, in fact, real.

The sense of touch is the sense of feeling, and God can both touch and be touched. We read, for example, of *"a band of men, whose hearts God had touched"* (I Samuel 10:26). In Hebrews 4:15, it states that "Jesus was not a high priest who cannot be touched with the feeling of our infirmities, but was in all points tempted like we are, yet without sin." Even people who never knew Him can perhaps *"seek Him and reach out for Him and find Him"* (Acts 17:27) if they truly desire His great salvation. In Acts 2:3, those who gathered in the upper room had "tongues of fire appear above their head." They must have sensed the heat of the fire on their heads!

Jesus was sensitive to the touch of the anointing of God in His life. In Mark 5:25-34, we read the story about the woman with the issue of blood. Jesus felt healing power flow out from Him when the woman touched Him, even though there were so many people touching Him in the crowd. The woman who was healed also felt the healing power flow into her as she realized what happened. Your heavenly Father also wants to open up the spiritual sense of touch to you so that you can tangibly feel His presence. When you feel His presence, He will download to you what He wants you to do so that you can partner with Him to do the works of His kingdom. How wonderful it is to come to the place of spiritual sensitivity where you can sense the power of God flowing through you as He uses you to pray for those who need healing, whether it be physical, spiritual or emotional healing.

Touch is so powerful, and sometimes it does something for you that no amount of words can do. For example, many times when I pray for someone who has lost a loved one, no amount of words can comfort them, but a hug speaks volumes. In such times, I always pray that this person will feel the tangible and comforting touch of God. Many times, when you pray and you need the touch of God, you may feel His loving touch envelope you.

Your sense of touch comes into play when your skin or scalp tingles or when you feel a pain that is meant to communicate a message to you. I am sure that sometimes when someone prays for you, you may feel the heat from this person's hands. It is God using this person's hands to touch you tangibly. Many people have been healed when healing anointing is evidently present. They testified that they feel the heat going through the part of their body that was being healed. The sense of touch is far more intimate than a smell. We are often touched by the presence of the Lord. Yet sometimes you may be touched in ways that are painful or scary. Being able to feel pain and to be touched by the suffering of yourself or others is critical in your life. Who among us, when touching a hot stove, doesn't immediately recoil and retreat to soothe the burn? It is a natural response to pain. You may be touched by a life that is ecstatic, peaceful, joyful, fearful, or painful. These are natural senses associated with a touch that sometimes God uses to communicate with you.

Sometimes the touch of God can be the feeling of peace as He covers you from head to toes. Have you ever been in a meeting where the presence of God is so strong that you feel His touch on you and you begin to laugh at the enemy? I had this experience once when I was carrying many burdens in my personal life. The speaker was used by God to touch me. I was anointed by him, and I fell under the power of the Holy Spirit and started laughing uncontrollably. When I stopped laughing, it was as if all my burdens were lifted away. I started to feel joy again (laughter is the overflow of joy). Within a short period, my situation was completely changed. Only the God of impossibilities can do this, and I was able to laugh at the enemy because no plans of the enemy can prevail against me.

There are many people who operate in the gift of knowledge who feel some pain physically in their body even though they do not have an affliction at all. If there is someone who needs healing in a part of the body, they will feel pain in that same part of their own body. The Spirit of God is saying to them, "There is someone in this meeting tonight who has that exact pain in their body, and I want to heal them!" Through the word of knowledge and through the sense of touch, they are able to stand up and describe what they are feeling in their body. The release of the word of knowledge allows those in need of healing to be ministered to for His glory.

May your prayer be that your heavenly Father would touch your heart for His glory. May He touch you deep within and bring you into a more intimate and personal relationship with Him. When He touches your heart, may He touch the core of your being and bring a real connection with Him and rekindle within you a longing for Him and His loving presence.

Activation of the sense of touch

1. Close your eyes. Imagine in your mind a honeydew melon and you are touching the skin. What does the skin feel like?

2. Read Isaiah 66:13: "As a mother comforts her child, so will I comfort you." Now close your eyes and ask the Holy Spirit to let you feel the heavenly Father touching and comforting you.

5. Through the spiritual sense of taste

The spiritual sense of taste is not as common, but it can still feel real to you. The sense of taste and smell go together. Your sense of taste can confirm a smell. The word taste comes from the Hebrew word "Ta'am," which means to savor, to experience. The spiritual sense of taste includes the taste of bitterness, sweetness, sourness, or saltiness. God can use any of the taste sensations to draw your attention to a particular issue that He wants to address in you or in a particular person. When you think of words to describe the taste, you have words such as amazing, appetizing, delightful, enticing, exquisite, divine, luscious, delicious, sweet, savory, yummy, scrumptious, lip-smacking, and spicy. Yet, how often do we use such beautiful words to describe an experience that we have with God or when we are reading the Bible?

David in Psalm 34:8 says, *"O taste and see that the Lord is good. Blessed is the man who trusts in Him."* David is reminding us that to taste the Lord, we need to trust him. The more we trust Him the more we can taste and see that He is good.

Psalm 119:103 says, *"How sweet are your words to my taste, sweeter than honey to my mouth."* Psalm 19:10 described the law of the Lord as, *"They are more desirable than gold, yes than much fine gold, sweeter than honey and the drippings of the honeycomb."*

When you taste something, you take it into yourself and it becomes part of you. You can see, touch, or hear something without it necessarily becoming a part of you. However, when you taste something it becomes part of you because you ingest it into your body. You transform it into your own being and your own flesh. In the same way, as you taste the Lord, you take Him as nourishment and food into your spirit and your spirit is transformed by it. No wonder Jesus says during the last supper to *"eat His body and to drink of His blood"* (Matthew 26:26-28). This is the way God wants to come into your life. He does not want to remain on the outside as something external to you. He wants to become a part of you because you ingest Him into your body, and He comes into your being. He does this through His Word, Jesus, who lives inside of you. Taste, therefore, is a way in which the presence of the Trinity becomes a reality to you, through you, and by you.

Ezekiel and John both received a vision in which they were given a scroll to eat. Ezekiel wrote, *"So I ate it, and it tasted as sweet as honey on my mouth"* (Ezekiel. 3:1-3). John received a scroll from an angel, and he wrote, *"It tasted as sweet as honey in my mouth, but when I had eaten it, my stomach turned sour"* (Revelations 10:8-10). In Jeremiah 15:16, Jeremiah said, *"When Your words came, I ate them, they were my joy and my heart's delight for I bear Your name, O Lord God Almighty."*

Kenneth MacDonald in his book, *Prophetic Seminar Handbook*, wrote:

> *If my spiritual father tastes gold in his mouth, he may say, 'I sense the true word of the Lord is here. Someone has it and it is in their mouth now.' Or it could be pointing to a provision, like the story of the gold coin in the fish's mouth. Use a biblical context to help interpret these impressions. If he tastes brass in his mouth, he may say, 'I sense judgment.' Brass is a symbol of judgment. Straw taste in the mouth can also mean judgment or hardship. If you smell straw in your place of business, it could mean that hardship is coming.*

Have you ever heard someone say, "That just leaves a bad taste in my mouth"? Some people have been known to taste fresh rain or felt the mist on their tongue during worship. During one of my training sessions that I was conducting, one of the participants said she felt a sudden bitterness on her tongue when she was praying for someone. God was showing her that the person has either gone through a bitter experience or was feeling bitter about a situation he had faced.

Activation for the sense of taste

1. Imagine that you are taking some cough mixture. What does it taste like?

2. Imagine that you are eating bitter gourd. What does it taste like?

3. Imagine that you are eating a piece of grapefruit. What does it taste like?

4. Imagine that you are swallowing a spoonful of honey. What does it taste like?

5. Imagine that you have just drank some milk that has gone bad. What does it taste like?

6. Imagine that you are eating some anchovies. What does it taste like?

7. Imagine that you are speaking some bitter words to someone that you are very angry with. How do the bitter words taste on your tongue when you speak?

Exercise to activate your five physical senses.

Now let me give you an exercise so you can experience all five physical senses.

Close your eyes. Imagine in your mind that you are stretching out both of your hands and imagine that I am handing you a pineapple. As I hand you the pineapple, see yourself touching the skin of the pineapple. What does the skin feel like? Next, imagine that I am giving you a knife to cut the pineapple. As you cut through the hard pineapple, what sound do you hear as the knife cuts through it? Can you smell the aroma emanating from the pineapple? Now I want you to imagine taking a piece of that pineapple and putting it in your mouth and tasting it. What does it taste like? Now open your eyes. Did you experience the five physical senses of sight, hearing, touch, smell, and taste, even though you have only imagined the pineapple in your mind?

Another exercise that you can try—Imagine you are walking through the park on your way to a café. Can you hear the wind rustling through the branches and the chirping of the birds? Can you see and smell the beautiful flowers and the freshness of the crisp air? As you touch the bark of the trees, can you feel the roughness of the bark? As you enter the café, can you smell the aroma of freshly brewed coffee and feel the anticipation of having some? (I am sure that by now, you would just want to go to the park and the cafe to experience all these five physical senses).

Now imagine that it's your birthday. Close your eyes. Imagine that you see the birthday cake, and everyone is singing the "Happy Birthday" song to you. Hear this in your imagination. Now imagine yourself blowing out the candles. Can you feel the heat from the candles and smell the burning wax? Next, imagine cutting a piece of your birthday cake and tasting it as it melts into your mouth. You have just experienced the five physical senses.

Exercise to activate your five spiritual senses

Now let me give you an exercise for you to experience the five spiritual senses. The Bible says in Zephaniah 3:17 that "God will rejoice over us with singing." Close your eyes and ask God to let you hear what He is singing over you. Ask Him to let you see the lyrics. Ask Him to let you smell His fragrance. Ask Him to let you feel His touch. Ask Him to let you taste His sweetness. In case you feel that this is weird, just remember that when He speaks to us, sometimes He uses all of our spiritual senses at once to communicate.

I have done this exercise with various groups of people and a number of them have testified that the songs that they hear are songs that they already know. For some, the tune of the song is the same, but the lyrics are different. For others, they hear a new tune and new lyrics which are completely new, a song they have never heard before. We call this the "new song." Many times, I have used this technique with people who are feeling discouraged and sad because it helps them to quiet their spirit and allow God to sing over them. Many of them have heard the singing, read the lyrics, felt His touch, the scent of His fragrance, and tasted His love and sweetness. Some of them are brought to tears as they sense so much love from the heavenly Father during their times of discouragement.

I strongly encourage you to do this activation exercise and you will be surprised at what He is singing over you. He will sing a different song in different seasons of your life. When you let Him touch you at the very heart in such an intimate way, you will never be the same again.

Prayer to offer and dedicate your five spiritual senses to God

For those who still fear that they may not be hearing from God but hearing their own voice/imagination or the enemy's voice, the prayers below will help to allay such fears.

"Dear Lord, I offer and dedicate myself, all the parts of my body and my five spiritual senses, to You as an instrument of righteousness. By faith, I receive an impartation right now from the Holy Spirit for my eyes of understanding to be enlightened and for greater vision in the spirit realm. I give You my imagination. I repent of and renounce viewing any image that has polluted me. I ask You to blot out every negative image with the blood of Jesus. Purify and restore my imagination. Restore the screen, vision, and revelation of my imagination. I ask that You open the unseen realm to me and remove all doubt, fear, wrong theology, and wrong mindset from my heart. I want to experience the fullness of all my spiritual senses. Please activate them to greater levels and help me to develop a sensitivity to You. Give me eyes to see, ears to hear, a nose to smell, a tongue to taste the things of God, and sensitivity to the sense of touch. I bring every thought of my mind and soul into captivity to the mind of Christ. When I receive an impression, thought, or word from the Holy Spirit within me, help me to not doubt or question it. I am a believer and I expect to be able to communicate with You through my five spiritual senses. I thank You that I will receive an impression, thought or word from Your throne room. In Jesus' name. Amen.

The command for binding the enemy's voice

For those of you who still feel afraid that you may be hearing the enemy's voice instead of the voice of God, you can command and forbid the enemy from imitating God's voice. You can say the command below:

"In the name of Jesus, by His power and authority, I take authority over every demon and interfering spirit and I forbid any enemy activity. Satan (or any of your demons), you may not interfere or imitate God's voice to me as I open my heart to hear Him. I take authority over fear, anxiety, doubt, and unbelief and in the name of Jesus, I command you to leave now."

Step-by-step practical exercise on how to commence your amazing adventure in hearing God's voice

After praying the above prayers, relax because this is about you having fun. Isn't it fun when you connect with your best friend? Connecting with God and having a conversation with Him is a thousand times more fun and exciting. Now go "down inside" and open your inner ears and eyes to receive the grace to start off.

1. Begin by asking God a question and anticipating an answer from Him. Ask the Lord to show you something in your imagination and ask Him what the picture means.

2. Pray in the Spirit in tongues or in your native language.

3. Keep quiet and listen/see/sense what information presents in your mind's eye.

4. Write down/draw anything that comes to your mind without trying to figure out whether it is really from God. Remember that it cannot be from the enemy as he has been forbidden to interfere with you. It also cannot be your thoughts as you have already prayed that every thought of your mind and soul is captive to the mind of Christ.

5. He may speak conversationally. Write down what He says.

6. He may cause you to recall verses or bring a portion of Scripture to your memory and if so, write it down.

7. He may show you a picture. If so, draw it or describe it.

8. You may be overcome with the sensation of joy or peace. Spend a few minutes enjoying it.

9. If you think that you are not hearing anything from God, then jot down whatever thoughts are going through your mind.

10. Sometimes it may help to take a step of faith and write these words, "Lord, I believe You are saying/showing this to me…" Begin to step out in faith and fill in whatever thoughts come to your mind. Place no limitations or expectations on what you write. Just let your pen flows with what you hear/see/sense.

11. When you think that you are done, ask God if there is anything else He would like to say to you.

12. Invite the Lord to be involved with you in the process of sorting out what you have written. Cross out anything that is unscriptural, or that contradicts the Bible and anything that is harsh and condemning (you will know that this is not from God). Note that sometimes you may be so used to hearing critical things that your default mode is "critical" in whatever you think. Just remember that this type of thought is from your own voice.

13. Go over what you have written and prayerfully read it again. It is very likely that God will give you more details as you ask Him more questions in order to have clarity. Enjoy the dialogue with Him as it is not so much about you trying to get answers to your questions, but about you getting to know Him more intimately.

Remember that God's word to you is always full of love, grace, and mercy because He loves you and has already planned a great future for you.

Examples of questions that you can ask God

Below are examples of questions you can ask God. You can ask Him any question on your heart. Feel free to ask Him further questions and remember this is not meant to be a one-way conversation but a dialogue with your heavenly Father who loves you. He may, in turn, ask you some questions as well. Have fun because communicating/connecting with your heavenly Father is supposed to be a fun, stress-free, and life-changing experience. Please also remember that the Holy Spirit is the Spirit of revelation and that He will be able to reveal to you what the Father is saying to you.

1. Heavenly Father, can You please show me/tell me/let me sense what you want to say to me about Your love for me?

2. Heavenly Father, can You please show me/tell me/let me sense what Your thoughts about me were when You were creating me in my mother's womb?

3. Heavenly Father, can You please show me /tell me/ let me sense what You are doing in my life now?

4. Heavenly Father, please show me/tell me/let me sense which actions of mine bring You delight?

Prayer

Dear heavenly Father, please help me to be open to the many ways that You use to speak to me. Help me to never put You in a box and dictate the way that You can speak to me. Please help me to take the step of faith and please hold my hands as You bring me on this amazing adventure of hearing Your voice. Help me to be sensitive to You so that whatever method that You use to speak to me, I will be able to discern Your voice. In Jesus' name. Amen.

Activation exercises

1. Dear heavenly Father, please show me in a picture Your thoughts on what I am going through now.

2. Dear heavenly Father, please let me hear what You are saying to me about this worry I have about a situation that I am going through.

3. Dear heavenly Father, please let me experience the taste of Your goodness in my life.

4. Dear heavenly Father, I know that you are always with me. Can You please let me smell Your fragrance?

5. Read John 5:1-8 and ask the Holy Spirit to reveal this to you in vision form and to give you a picture in your mind that matches this scene. Do the same for Daniel 10:5,6 and Acts 10:11. Ask the Holy Spirit to show you what the vision looks like.

SUMMARY

The way that God speaks to you is so varied and creative. You must not put God in a box. You must learn to be open when He changes His channel of communication. No one way of receiving communication from God is superior to another. You must allow yourself to learn to develop all spiritual senses. The more you exercise your spiritual senses, the more you will become effective and efficient in the use of these senses.

The willingness to obey every word from God is critical to hearing God speak.

—Henry T. Blackaby, *Hearing God's Voice*

8
WHAT DO YOU DO WITH WHAT YOU HAVE HEARD FROM GOD?

Many of us love to receive a prophetic word from God, be it directly from Him or from someone else. However, not many of us know what to do with the prophetic word from God. Below is some advice on what to do with the prophetic words that you have received.

1. Write it down. Do not rely on your memory.

When you receive a word from God, you may not think to write it down in a journal, type it on a computer, or save it as a note on your phone. You may assume that you will always remember what God said to you. However, as the days go by, the message will get fainter and fainter and eventually you will reach a point when you can't even remember what He said. You cannot depend on your memory to recall the prophetic word and therefore it's important to write it down. When you don't keep a record of the prophetic word, it is, in a way, telling God that you do not really treasure the words He has spoken to you. May you be like Mary, who *"treasured all these things in her heart"* (Luke 2:19). The "things" refer to what the angel, Gabriel, the shepherds and her cousin, Elizabeth had told Mary. When you read the Old Testament about the Israelites, how often do the words "they forgot" appear in the Scripture (Psalm 10:21, Judges 8:34)? We may think we are not like the Israelites, but as human beings, many times we do behave like them.

A good way of recording your encounters and experiences with God is journaling. Journaling is not a one-way communication (like writing in a diary). Journaling is useful for memory recalls, helps to clarify thinking and understanding yourself and your relationships with God and the people around you.

Journaling helps you to remember God's word that is spoken to you, and the various events in our life. You record God's faithfulness when God helped you through the difficult times and the victories in Christ through the years. It is a good resource to refer back to when you are feeling down or trying to solve problems or check in on your relationship with God. You can use your journal to review, to clarify in your mind, to prioritize, and to accomplish the things of God. You can tell your heavenly Father what's in your heart—your deepest fears, your dreams, and desires. You must be honest and authentic in your writing and be led by the Holy Spirit, as you write down what you feel God is saying to you. You will discover that as you write down what God shows you, other spontaneous thoughts may surface. This can happen when you allow the Holy Spirit to take over your writing. As you write, your dreams, desires, and deepest longings may begin to enter your writing and become clearer to you. When you read and reflect on what you've written, you may find that He is giving you a reply or solution for your situation. God wants to reveal more of Himself and His ways as you continue to communicate with Him and co-operate with Him. The journaling process is certainly an excellent way of building intimacy with your heavenly Father.

The journals can serve as a memento, not only for yourself but also for the next generation to know about God's faithfulness to you. Sometimes you can use your journaling to write a blog to encourage others who are going through the same situation. You may even write a book as a legacy of God's faithfulness in your life. So, journaling helps you to remember clearly what exactly has happened, for it is very easy to forget revelations and experiences as time passes by.

Scott Stanley and Brandon Wood, in their book *The Voice of God*, compared journaling using paper and pen versus using the computer. They wrote:

> It is our experience that God prefers paper and pen. He actually told Scott that paper and pen are more intimate than a computer. When Scott tried to use a computer, he heard nothing. He then went to his journal and God gave him three pages of text. It may be different with you, but we highly recommend a notebook and pen.

Writing down helps you to respond to God as you open your heart and initiate the dialogue with Him. You can begin to ask Him for more clarification. It also gives you the opportunity to wait on Him. When you write down and record your deepest thoughts, this can also help you to journal your thankfulness, hopes, dreams, goals, fears, and concerns. He longs to give you more revelation, if only you will take the time to ask Him. His dream for you can only become a reality if you partner with Him.

Mark Virkler in his book, *Hearing God through Biblical Meditation* wrote:

> Anything God says to you will be in harmony with His essential nature. Journaling will help you get to know God personally but knowing what the Bible says about Him will help you discern what words are from Him. They will represent His very nature. Even though the details of what you are journaling may not be specifically expressed in Scripture, the essence of what God is revealing to you will always be in agreement with His attributes. Make sure the tenor of your journaling lines up with the character of God as described in the names of the Father, Son, and Holy Spirit.

Keith A. Paul in his book, *Prophecy: Stepping into the Prophetic Realm*, gave this advice regarding journaling:

> Write down what He is saying and be receptive as He will use

the same faculties of communication that we would use in the natural. We are then positioning ourselves for the Holy Spirit to download prophetic encounters on us.

2. Test the prophetic word by comparing what is written in Scripture.

You need to avoid the mistake of thinking God's voice is your thoughts or imagination and thus dismissing it even before you have weighed it properly. On the flip side, you also need to learn to avoid the mistake of thinking everything that comes to your mind is from God or from Satan. You hear God more than you give yourself credit for. The extreme of thinking everything that comes to your mind is from God can result in deception and pride. In Thessalonians 5:19-21, Paul instructed the church not to treat prophecies with contempt, but to examine everything carefully, to hold fast to what is good, and to avoid every form of evil. The prophetic word must conform to the teachings in Scripture and must be in line with the character of God and His values. The prophetic word speaks to men for their strengthening, encouragement, and comfort (1 Corinthians 14:3).

According to Les D. Crause in his book, *The Prophetic Warfare*, there are three things that you can judge, or weigh or assess regarding what you hear. These are: (a) the nature and character of God and the values upon which His Kingdom is built (b) the heart of God for mankind and (c) Scripture—the overall tenet of Scripture, not just individual proof verses.

He further gave this advice: *"True communication from God will not contradict those three things. If you are not sure what you are hearing is from God, don't be afraid to invite mature Christians to offer their discernment and counsel. It is always wise to walk in accountability."*

3. Ask for clarity if the prophetic word is not clear.

You can ask God whether the prophetic word is for now or in the future or whether it is a new word or a confirming word. You can also ask God for clarification and for the timing. You can ask God whether there are any pre-requisites you must fulfill or preparation that you must do before the prophetic word can come to pass. Do not just ignore the prophetic word or think that it's your imagination or say it's from the devil. You should value the word of God even though you may not understand how it applies to your life right now. For example, in Luke 2:19, when the angel appeared before Mary and told her that she would bear a child of the highest God, I'm sure she did not fully understand all that was involved. However, the Bible states that she *"treasured this in her heart."*

When God speaks in response to your question, you need to realize it is a conversation/dialogue that you are having with Him. If there are some answers which are not clear to you, you are free to ask Him for clarification or ask Him another question based on the answers He's given you. He wants you to have a dialogue with Him. He is not like your earthly parents who sometimes get frustrated when they are asked too many questions. God is the ever-patient Father who will not be angry, even if you ask Him the same questions many times, especially when you are not sure whether you've heard Him correctly and accurately. He will bring clarity when you ask Him more questions. It's just like having a conversation with a friend. You ask God a question and then He answers, and you ask Him another question and so on. It's just as natural for you to converse with your heavenly Father as it is when you are speaking with your earthly parents or your friends. You do not need to worry about running out of topics to talk to Him about. You will find that the more you converse with Him, the more you will know Him and His character. This is how you build intimacy with Him. Examples of dialogues that God had with the Israelites are recorded in Malachi (1:2-3; 6-8, 2:17, 3:6-8, 13-15). You will find that the Israelites asked God questions and God, in turn, asked them questions too.

4. Ask God for the interpretation and application of the prophetic word you have received.

When you receive a prophetic word from God, don't make the mistake of believing that what you have received was a complete communication. You may not think of asking God for more details if you are not aware that receiving a word or revelation from God is only the beginning of the process of God speaking. You must also understand that there are three parts to a prophetic word you receive. The three parts are: (a) the revelation itself (b) the interpretation (c) the application.

Many people who have learned to hear God's voice are eager to give prophetic words when they receive the revelation. However, many people stop short of asking God for the interpretation and the application. The revelation is complete only when these three elements are combined together. The revelation is the actual insight you receive from God through the means of the prophetic word. For example, you may see a picture or hear a word or have a God-thought or sensing from God. You can make the mistake of stopping at this point and failing to ask God for the interpretation. All revelation from God is an invitation to intimacy and relationship. Write the word from God in as much detail as you can remember so that you can spend time waiting on Him for the interpretation.

The interpretation involves discovering the meaning of the revelation. You can ask Him for more details, for example, you can ask Him the what, why, how, when, who, and where type of questions. You can ask Him whether the revelation is literal or symbolic. If it is symbolic, then ask Him what it symbolizes. You should not be afraid to ask God about any detail if it is unclear to you. He is a loving Father and He will give you the interpretation if you ask Him. Don't worry, He will not get angry or upset or impatient with you. It is very important not to use your own understanding to figure out what the revelation means as you could very well end up with the wrong interpretation. Remember you have the Holy Spirit to ask and He will lead you into all truth (John 16:13).

Once you have received the interpretation from the Holy Spirit, you need to ask God how you should apply this. This may involve you taking action because the application is the outworking of the revelation and interpretation. You can start by asking Him how to implement what He has said to you, i.e. ask Him for the blueprint. You can ask Him more questions to get greater clarity and more details. The implementation may well require you to do something that you have never done before. You should not be frightened by the instructions

WHAT DO YOU DO WITH WHAT YOU HAVE HEARD FROM GOD? 159

that you receive from Him. Just remember God is creative, and He will give you directions and ideas that are so creative that your own natural understanding and wisdom could never have thought of it. You should ask Him to breathe His creativity, wisdom, and counsel into you so you can complete the application step with tangible actions.

Sometimes due to ignorance or having a "can't be bothered to ask for more" attitude, many of us may skip the step of asking God for the interpretation and application when we receive the revelation. I always tell my trainees to stretch themselves and to keep on asking for more from God and to not be satisfied to just have a vision from God. Those who followed this advice were very excited to receive the full revelation, which gave them the clarity on what to do and when, etc. Just stopping at revelation and interpretation without application is likened to being pregnant with the prophetic word but never taking care of the pregnancy and in the end, never giving birth at all. Thus, the prophetic words you receive may end up being a miscarriage or a stillbirth because nothing was done to apply what was heard from God. The result is not fulfilling the destiny God has planned for you.

Rod Christensen in the book, *Prophetic Streams*, gave a definition of revelation and what revelation does for you:

> *Revelation is the spontaneous, instant insight from the Lord, disclosing Heaven's perspective on a matter formerly outside of our present understanding, perception, and frame of reference. The effect of revelation is like when we turn on a light switch and the light rays drive away the darkness so that what was concealed and beyond our perception, becomes recognizable. The Holy Spirit uses revelation to shine forth the light of God into our hearts so that we can see correctly. Through these experiences, the Lord begins to incubate change within us and changes our frame of reference. One of the amazing characteristics of God is His ability to create something from nothing. When the Lord initiates revelation, there is deposited within our hearts the seed of destiny. He does it this way, so we can be involved and even co-operate with His creative process.*

An example of using revelation, interpretation, and application.

I will give an example of a vision that I had to explain the three steps of revelation, interpretation, and application.

Recently I was praying for a lady who had a relapse of sickness in her body. As I prayed for her, I saw a picture of a big mountain. What was strange about this mountain was that there was a door at the base of the mountain. The door could be opened, allowing one to walk through to the other side of the mountain, into an open space which was lush and green. As I released this revelation to the lady, I asked the Holy Spirit for the interpretation. The interpretation was that though this lady was facing a mountain where health was concerned, God had created a door for her to go through the mountain supernaturally. No one constructs a door through a mountain; normally people climb up, over and then down the mountain, in order to get to the other side. However, what God had prepared for this precious lady was a door to go right through this mountain. God was going to help her through this health issue, not in the normal way, but in a supernatural way. The greatest assurance and comfort were that God was going through the mountain with her as she would not be able to do this in her own strength. The application for this dear sister was to take the vision given and believe and declare that she would go through the mountain with God by her side. She *will* go through and end up on the other side. She will overcome the mountain that she is facing for God has created a supernatural way for her to go through it. Therefore, when doubt arises or discouragement comes like a wave, this vision will help her to declare that in the natural, it may seem difficult and impossible for her to go through this health issue, but God has already created a way for her. She will not be alone while going through this difficult experience. This vision can then be used to war against the enemy when doubts arise, for she can now declare that she will not only go through the mountain but come out victorious. Praise God!

5. Meditate and pray over the prophetic word you have received.

Once you have tested the word against Scripture and confirmed that the source is from God, you need to hold on to these words like treasures. You should meditate on the words and on Scripture and ask the Holy Spirit to reveal and explain the meaning and relevance to you. Joshua was instructed to meditate on the word of God day and night and to be careful to obey every word that God had commanded him to do (Joshua 1:8).

If you treasure what God has said to you, you will meditate and pray over it and then come back to the *Rhema* word (spoken word of God) time and time again. You cannot pray over the Rhema word that He has spoken to you if you have not previously written it down somewhere. I've heard it said that you will eventually lose 95% of what you have heard if you don't write it down. No doubt, the Holy Spirit can bring to memory what God has spoken to you, but how much better to write it down so that you can re-visit it again and again. You will find that if you re-visit and meditate on what God has spoken to you, there will be more clarity and even more revelation. By doing this, it will also help to build up your faith. This is because when you first hear His *Rhema* word, your faith is at a super high level. However, your faith level can slowly dwindle away over time, if what was spoken has still not come to pass. You start to question whether you have heard correctly from Him in the first place. This is especially so when you are going through a trial and your situation appears to be the opposite of the prophetic word that you had received. Reading what God has said will ignite your faith once again. If you did not write down God's words, you may be living and acting as if He has never spoken to you at all. When you think of Joseph's dream and the timeframe in which it was fulfilled, you cannot help but ask how many times Joseph must have wondered whether his dream would ever come to pass.

6. Honor the prophetic word (what God has spoken to you or through someone else).

As you honor the prophetic word of God through prayer, it helps you to bring your spirit in agreement and alignment with what God has spoken over you. Your faith level will need to rise in order for the word to be fulfilled. You are then able to use the prophetic word to war against any doubts that the enemy tries to throw at you. As you continually remember in prayer the prophetic word God has given, it will help you to fight against the feeling of discouragement. When you honor the prophetic word, you give the Holy Spirit your permission to help you fulfill the potential in your life. The Holy Spirit then begins to transform your thoughts and mind to align it with the thoughts that your heavenly Father has for you. You will begin to speak and see yourself the way God sees and thinks about you. It is like you projecting His thoughts into your mind until His thoughts for you are superimposed on your thoughts. You continue to do this until His thoughts become your thoughts. You will begin to treasure the prophetic word given to you and make the effort, not only to reflect on it, but also to obey it. If you are passionate about receiving prophetic words over your life, then you should also be passionate about obeying the prophetic word. This is because every prophetic word has an element of obedience in order for it to be fulfilled. The enemy will try to put obstacles and discouragement along your way to hinder you from fulfilling our destiny.

Like David and Joseph, you need to persevere and push through what God has said, no matter how difficult it is or how long it will take. You must remember that God has a plan for your life. He wants to give you life more abundantly (John 10:10). Satan also has a plan for your life and his plan is to kill, steal, and destroy all that God has planned for you. Many times, after a prophetic word is given, everything seems to go the exact opposite of what the prophetic word said. Suddenly you have the attention of Satan and he is on the onslaught to hinder you from fulfilling what the prophetic word says. Satan will use every weapon he has to try to hijack and derail your prophetic word. This is the reason why it is important to fight the good fight using the Rhema word that was given to you. You must use this as your spiritual weapon against doubt, discouragement, unbelief, and fear. As you recall, recite, and meditate on the prophetic word over your life, you will begin to see with your spiritual eyes and hear with your spiritual ears what God is saying about your potential. Many prophetic words get "lost" and it is likened to a seed that is kept aside but not planted in faith and watered with the declaration from the word of God

WHAT DO YOU DO WITH WHAT YOU HAVE HEARD FROM GOD? 163

7. Obey what the prophetic word tells you to do.

Many people run around to prophetic conferences and spirit-filled meetings receiving and giving words to each other without really walking out the destiny God has for them. God wants more for you than to just give you a "good" word to make you feel good. When God gives you a prophetic word, He wants something to happen. However, there is always a pre-requisite that is attached to it. Believing that the prophetic word will come to pass is just the first step. May you be someone who not only believes God but also obeys what He asks you to do. When you are meditating on the prophetic word given to you, you need to examine your actions constantly and ask yourself, "What did I do with the last word that was spoken to me? Did I obey it and do something with it?"

A prophetic word speaks to your potential. When you are faced with the reality of the current situation and the potential that God says about you, make the decision to believe what He says instead of what you may see with your natural eyes. Then ask Him for His wisdom to prepare you so that you can walk into your destiny. Conversely, you can read the prophetic word He gave you, and with a heart full of doubt and fear, decide not to do anything about it. God is a gentleman and He will not force you to do something that you do not want to do. However, when you are prepared to make the changes that He wants you to make, He will engineer the circumstances in your life to prepare you to be able to fulfill your destiny.

God will rarely give you something new until you have acted upon or obeyed the last thing that He told you to do. If you want to increase your sensitivity in hearing His voice, you need to develop an attitude of immediate obedience, no matter how inconvenient or difficult it may seem. Obedience is the greatest way to honor the voice of God. To obey Him may mean you must get rid of things in your life that are not in agreement and alignment with the prophetic destination that He has given you. You must begin to make choices and decisions which are now consistent with the destiny He has prepared for you, no matter how you feel or the doubt in your mind. You must make the conscious choice to go towards the destination God has shown you and make the decision to leave behind those things which hinder or distract you from moving forward towards your destiny. May you be like Joshua, who was able to walk into his destiny because he obeyed the instructions and commands of God.

In my own personal life, the writing of this book is in obedience to what the heavenly Father asked me to do in 2015. Initially, I did not embrace the calling and "conveniently" put it into the "too hard to do" basket. I had many excuses, including that I had just begun a job which was very demanding. Towards the end of my first year in the new job, I asked God what He wanted me to do in 2016. He gently reminded me that He had asked me to write a book. There was no condemnation in His voice, but His gentle voice made me want to do this to obey Him and to please Him. It was a tough decision to obey Him as there were many sacrifices to be made. The flesh wants to rest after a hard day of work and the flesh wants to relax on the weekend. However, as I remembered His calling to me to write the book, I could not but do it as a pleasing sacrifice and offering to Him.

I love what Jim Goll wrote in his book, *The Coming Prophetic Revolution*:

> *Few words are declarations that something will automatically come into being. Most words are invitations to respond to God with conditions that must be met first. Few prophetic words are immediate or 'now' words. Most help us in the process of becoming. Few prophetic words get us out of a dilemma. They are used to shed light, comfort and encourage us to continue on. There are no 'shortcuts' with God! Focus not on the promise but on the God who promised. Realize the clarity and cost equation. What God counts as significant will often arouse great opposition by the enemy. Every promise contains a cost. Give room for "time-lapse." As most invitations are towards an end, there is a duration of time in between while the person is being prepared for the promise that is on the way.*

8. When doubts come, you need to go back to the prophetic word.

John the Baptist was told by God in John 1:33, *"He upon whom you see the Spirit descending and remaining upon Him, this is the one who baptizes in the Holy Spirit."* However, when John the Baptist was put in prison by Herod, he started having doubts about what God has told him about Jesus being the Son of God. He sent his disciples to ask Jesus *"whether He is the Expected One (Messiah) or should they expect someone else"* (Matthew 11:2). When your faith is being tested and you are facing extreme circumstances, you may be like John where you start to question what you previously knew to be the true word from God. It is very easy for you to be full of doubts when what you have received from God does not come to pass in your expected time frame.

When you doubt whether the prophetic word will ever come to pass, you must remember that God is bigger than what you could ever imagine. There will be the argument in your mind that you cannot do what He has called you to do based on experiences that you've had or what other people have said to you. This, in turn, becomes your belief system. As you reflect on the prophetic word, the false beliefs and limitations that you have put on yourself become clear. This helps you to go to your heavenly Father in prayer to seek His help to remove the obstacles of your unbelief so that you can fulfill what He has called you to do.

9. Use the prophetic word to build an altar as a memorial.

In the Old Testament, the people of God built an altar as a memorial whenever something significant happened in their lives. For example, Abraham (Genesis 12:7-8), Isaac (Genesis 26:25), and Jacob (Genesis 33:20 35:1-7) did this. When the Israelites crossed over the Jordan River, God asked them to bring twelve stones from the river and build a memorial so that their children could remember what God had done. Wouldn't it be awesome if you could leave for your children, not just a financial inheritance, but also your journal as a memorial of God's faithfulness in your life? You must not let your next generation be like the Israelites who grew up but did not know anything of God or what He had done (Judges 2:10).

As for me, I record key moments in my journal when God has spoken to me. It could be victories that I have experienced or discouragement that I've gone through. As I look through my journal, I can testify that through it all, God has come through for me in every situation that I've faced. Each journey needs to be journaled so as to keep a record of the experience. When I feel discouraged and I am going through a similar situation again, I can read my previous journal and be encouraged that through it all, God is still in control and that His will for my life will prevail and that the enemy cannot thwart God's plans for my life.

As you write in the journal, it will also serve as a record of your emotional and spiritual growth. It will serve as a testimony of your life which you can share with others to encourage them. It is also a legacy that you can leave for future generations as it will be like a road map for them. This can be used to remind them that God does not change through the ages and what He has done for one generation, He can do likewise for another generation. God may also use your experiences with Him to bring encouragement and blessing to others so that they can walk in the reality of the same blessings that you have experienced. Your experiences can become a confirmation and an invitation to them to experience God at a deeper level and to know Him more intimately than they do at present.

10. You can use the prophetic word to check whether you are heading in the right direction over time.

Often times, when God gives you a prophetic word, it tells you the direction to take and the destination that you will reach. When you are going somewhere that you've never been before, you may ask someone for directions. That person may ask, "Do you have something to write this down?" (Because most people will forget the directions if they are not written down). In the busyness of life and with the passing of time, you may not remember much of the details unless it is written down. So, if you have recorded the prophetic word from the start, it's easy to refer to the notes to review and meditate on the word that He has given you. As you respond to His guidance, especially when you feel lost or in need of further clarification, God will lead you out of the wilderness and onto the right path.

11. You need to compare the prophetic word with other prophetic words that you have received previously.

Many times, when God speaks to you, you may not get the full understanding the first time you hear it. You may miss a lot of the details in the beginning because you may discredit it as your own imagination. God will often use someone to give you a prophetic word to confirm what He has previously spoken to you about.

You will notice in Deuteronomy 31:23 that Moses told Joshua to *"be strong and courageous."* In Joshua 1:7, God told Joshua to "*Be strong and very courageous.*" In Joshua 1:18, the Israelites told Joshua to "*Be strong and courageous.*" Why did Joshua need to hear the same words, "Be strong and courageous" from God and then again from two other different sources? It could be that there was a long lapse from when Moses commissioned Joshua to when he had to lead the Israelites into the Promised Land. Maybe during that time, Joshua had doubts along the way or maybe he forgot about the initial prophetic word spoken to him by Moses. God told Joshua the same thing three times (Joshua 1:6, 1:7 and 1:9) and He even used the words, "very courageous" in Joshua 1:7. As if that was not enough, God even used the Israelites to affirm the same thing to Joshua (Joshua 1:18). Joshua must have had major doubts concerning leading the Israelites into the Promised Land, even though he was commissioned by Moses. We must remember that years before Moses' death, God had already begun to prepare Joshua for the task of leading the people to inherit the Promised Land. When it was time for Joshua to finally take action, God told Joshua, *"Moses is dead. Now then, you and all these people, get ready to cross the Jordan River into the land I am about to give to the Israelites"* (Joshua 1:2). This was after the Israelites had mourned Moses' death for thirty days (Deuteronomy 34:8).

In many ways, you may be like Joshua. For example, you may be in a situation where God has told you what He will do. You are at peace for a little while, but a short time later, doubt starts to creep in, and you begin to wonder whether God has really told you what He will do. In such instances, God can use someone to give you another prophetic word which essentially says the same thing, especially if it is something that He does not want you to miss. The greater and the more difficult the assignment, the more times He will try to get the message across to you. He will patiently keep confirming what He has told you to do.

Sometimes you may think it's a coincidence and so you start to worry about your situation again. God, in His love and mercy, will use another person to tell you the same thing. For example, you may be in church hearing the Word being preached, and the preacher may use the same words God spoke to you previously. Even though God has spoken three times to you already, you may still have doubts in your heart.

God is so gracious and never gives up on you. Instead, He will always communicate with you so that you will not miss what He is saying. When you are in doubt if this is really God's word, receiving the same message many times from various sources serves as a confirmation that it is truly God's voice that you heard. So, when you hear a prophetic word from someone, compare it with what you have previously received from God. You may be surprised that God can speak the same message to you through a diversity of people and circumstances.

Prayer:

Dear heavenly Father, please forgive me for the many times I have not really paid much attention when You've spoken to me. I have not even bothered to write it down as I think that I will remember what You have said. I must admit that sometimes You seem to be telling me the same thing, but I've ignored it because, in my mind, it is just too hard to accomplish. I do not always put a value on what You have said to me, and frequently, I take our relationship and time together for granted.

Many times, I have failed to ask You for more clarity when I've received a word from You. I was afraid that You would get angry with me if I asked too many questions. I now know that this is not in line with Your character.

Please help me to wage warfare with the word that You have given to me. Even though it may seem as if it will never happen, help me to know in my spirit that every word that You have spoken will not return to You void, but will accomplish what You desire and achieve the purpose for which it was sent.

Help me to put into practice what I have learned so that I can begin the amazing adventure of hearing Your voice in every area of my life. I am looking forward to a more intimate and personal relationship with You. As I converse with You, I know that You will direct and guide me so that I can fulfill the destiny that You have for me. In Jesus' name. Amen.

Activation exercises

1. Holy Spirit, please bring to my memory a prophetic word that I have received previously that I may have forgotten. Show me what I need to do about that prophetic word.

2. Holy Spirit, please show me one thing that you want me to do that You have been repeating to me but that I have ignored. Bring this to my memory again and this time, I promise that I will write it down and ask You for more clarity.

3. Holy Spirit, there is a prophetic word that I have received, and life seems to be going the opposite to what You say will happen. As I quiet my spirit, please show me Your perspective regarding this and what I should do in preparation while waiting for the fulfillment of the prophetic word.

SUMMARY

You must remember to journal any prophetic word that you have heard from God. It is absolutely important that you test the prophetic word that you receive using Scripture. As you meditate and pray over the word received from the Lord, you should ask for clarity, if the prophetic word is not clear to you. You should also ask for the interpretation and application of the prophetic word. It is easy for you to doubt a prophetic word that seems to take a long time before it is fulfilled. In such a time, remember that every word spoken by God to you will definitely come to pass if you partner with Him and yield yourself to Him.

Unbelief can render a person stone deaf to God's voice.

—Henry T. Blackaby, *Hearing God's Voice*

❧ 9 ☙

POTENTIAL HINDRANCES IN HEARING GOD'S VOICE

In this chapter, I will cover some potential hindrances you may face in hearing God's voice, though this is not an exhaustive list. I use the word "hindrances" because nothing can stop your heavenly Father from speaking to you or stop you from hearing His voice. Just remember, even after Adam and Eve sinned, they could still hear God's voice when He called their names in the Garden of Eden. Even after Cain killed his brother, he could still hear God's voice. When God asked him, "Cain, where is your brother, Abel?" Cain answered God, "Am I my brother's keeper?" God will do whatever is necessary to speak to you because He loves you, and nothing can separate you from His love and His willingness to communicate with you.

Listed below are some reasons why you may have trouble hearing God's voice:

1. You think that the only way God speaks to you is through the Bible.

2. You don't believe that He still speaks to you today or that He is interested in speaking to you.

3. You're not paying attention to Him when He is speaking to you or you cannot discern when He is speaking to you.

4. You are allowing some kind of interference to drown out His voice in your life.

5. You do not know the frequency that He is speaking to you on and so you are unable to tune to that same frequency.

6. You are so used to a particular frequency when He speaks to you that when He changes that frequency, you are still tuned into the previous frequency.

Some common reasons why you may have difficulties in hearing His voice:

1. Doubt/disbelief

Jesus says in John 10:27, "*My sheep listen to my voice; I know them, and they follow me.*" There are some people who think that unless they have a prophetic gift or some other spiritual gift or special ministry, they cannot hear God's voice. Some people who are so convinced they cannot hear God and so they don't. Many people cannot and will not hear the voice of God in their lives because they simply do not believe God still speaks or that they are able to hear His voice. Whenever they hear someone say that they have heard from God, they roll their eyes and their inner thoughts will be something like: *Who do they think they are? They think they are so special. I think they are just making it up to make themselves seem important.* Let us be like David who says, "*In the morning, O Lord, you hear my voice; in the morning I lay my requests before you and wait in expectation*" (Psalm 5:3).

Though it is normal to have doubts about things that you have never experienced before, may you not stay in the place of unbelief. We should be like the father in Mark 9:24 who says, "I do believe. Help me overcome my unbelief." Unbelief will clog up your spiritual ability to hear, while faith will open it up. When you expect to hear His voice, you will hear for God will not disappoint you. When you approach the

Lord with the joyful expectation that you will hear His voice, then you will open all your spiritual senses to hear Him. For example, there are many people who have not experienced healing or the baptism of the Holy Spirit and therefore, they do not believe that this is for Christians today. I suppose for me, the greatest joy I experience when I conduct my training session is bringing someone from a place of doubt and disbelief to a place where they can hear God for themselves. Once they experience this, they will never be the same again, for now they have not just heard about it, but they have experienced it for themselves: God still speaks today. However, they require open hearts and faith to go from a place of doubt to a place of faith and truth. Many people are not even willing to open their hearts to this possibility, so they remain in this status quo year in and year out and sadly they never experience the fullness of what God has in store for them. You must remember not to bring your faith level down to the level of your experience, but instead, you must bring your experience level up to your faith level.

2. Fear of not being able to discern God, Satan, or your own voice

You need to overcome the fear of hearing from the wrong source. If you continue to fear that you will hear your own voice or Satan's voice, you will never begin your journey of hearing God's voice. It's important to have faith to believe that if you ask your loving Father to let you hear His voice, then He will not let you hear your own voice or Satan's voice. You must realize that God is more powerful than Satan and that He is able to prevent Satan from interfering or imitating His voice. You must learn to walk by faith and not by fear for God's perfect love for you will cast out all fear. If you ask God for something good, He is not going to give you something evil because He is a loving heavenly Father (Matthew 7:8-10; Luke 11:12-13). If you command and take captive every thought that you have and make it obedient to Christ (1 Corinthians 10:5), you can have the confidence and trust that your loving heavenly Father will let you hear His voice only. He will certainly help you to discern His voice from the other voices that you might be hearing.

3. Thinking that God only speaks to you through the Bible

You may have been told that you should not rely on your feelings, emotions, or experiences. You, therefore, live your Christian life by trying to confine your time with God based solely on what you read and without involving your emotions, feelings, or imagination. I am so glad Lyn Packer clearly explained the connection between relationship and experience in her book, *Visions, Visitations and the Voice of God*:

> *You cannot have a relationship without experience. Although we are not to worship experience itself, it is only by experience that we come to learn and know the one we are in a relationship with. We know each other by experiencing things together—good and bad; by talking, observing, and sharing our hearts with each other. For the last few centuries, many Western Christians lived their Christianity from a Greek mindset and point of view, instead of the Hebrew mindset that influenced the early Church. The Greek mindset infers, 'You know something when you understand it as it is.' The Hebrew mindset embraces the belief 'You don't truly know something until you experience and understand it.' God is bringing about a transformation of our minds in this hour, leading to the emergence of a truly supernatural Church rightly displaying who God is, because they have experienced who He is.*

If you think God can only speak to you through the Bible, then all Satan needs to do is to prevent you from reading the Bible and theoretically, that would prevent you from hearing God's voice. I am so glad that God is bigger and more creative than His love letter (the Bible). He will find ways to speak to you, even if you do not read the Bible. You may have heard the testimonies of Jesus appearing and speaking to non-Christians even though these people knew nothing about the Bible. Somehow, they knew it was Jesus who spoke to them. The God who loves you is infinitely creative and not limited by the way that you are used to communicating with Him.

4. Fear of the Holy Spirit

Many people are terrified of spiritual experiences because of what they have heard from others. Therefore, they reject the possibility of visitations from angels or from God. They also reject speaking in tongues and the gifts of the Spirit. They are very skeptical of anything that is spiritual or any mention of the Holy Spirit. Because they have never experienced hearing God's voice, they do not believe that He still speaks today or that the Holy Spirit's gifts are still available for all Christians. Many people who attend a traditional church may have been taught that the gifts of the Spirit have already ceased and are no longer in operation today. When the Holy Spirit speaks to them, they freak out and think they are out of their minds or that they are hearing from Satan.

5. Having difficulty being still so that you can hear His voice

We live in a world where we find it very difficult to be still either outwardly or inwardly. Sometimes you may be still outwardly, but your mind is racing at the speed of a thousand miles per hour.

Ryan Wyatt in *School of the Supernatural: Live the Supernatural Life that God Created You to Live* gave this advice on how to make your spirit the master of your mind when you are trying to be still.:

> *Becoming still remains the greatest challenge. If we are going to commune with God, first we must become still. Habakkuk went to his guard post to pray (see Habakkuk 2:1). In the early morning when it was still dark, Jesus departed to a lonely place to pray, and after a day's ministry, Jesus went to a mountain to pray (see Luke 9:28). They reduced the outward distractions around them. But what about inward distractions? Most believers are completely dominated by their minds. They can't stop their minds from working when they want. You must learn to beat your mind into subjection. Your spirit needs to become the master of your mind. One practical tip is this: if you think of things to do, write them down. Then say to your mind, 'You can't tell me things to do anymore. All my to-do list is written down, so be quiet.' (Obviously, if your sins come to mind, confess them and get rid of them. Then you can't blame that as a*

distraction anymore, either.) Your mind wants to be in charge. It wants to know what is going on and it wants to understand it, analyze it. If your mind wanders aimlessly, speak in tongues. Paul said, 'When I speak in tongues, my mind is unfruitful, but my spirit is speaking to the Lord' (1 Corinthians. 14:14). I am not just talking about doing this for five minutes. I would speak in tongues for hours until my mind completely gave up and I didn't even know what I was doing anymore. It was great because my mind learned who was boss. Speaking in tongues energizes your spirit. It causes your spirit to open up. It sensitizes your spirit.

6. Using your reasoning to question what you have heard

Your ability to hear God's voice may be hindered when you use logical or analytical thinking or your natural reasoning process. This will result in you finding reasons to reject what God says because you "don't understand it" or "it just doesn't make sense," or it seems "illogical."

One of my friends, Pat L, shared about a dilemma she was facing in having to decide whether she should apply for her own job or take the redundancy (severance package) that was being offered to her. She asked me for advice. In my natural reasoning and based on what I have seen and heard about the economic situation, I told her that the best option seemed to be for her to take the redundancy package. However, I cautioned her to ask God for herself because she shouldn't base such an important decision on what others think or even on a prophetic word. I am so glad that she sought God for herself because she later told me that God spoke very clearly to her three times not to take the redundancy package.

When she was given the opportunity to apply for her job again, God reminded her of what He'd told her. She went for the interview and found that nearly two hundred applicants had applied for the job. Many applicants were also younger and more highly qualified than her. Guess what? She got the job! So human reasoning and logic can sometimes hinder what God wants to do in your life because it often seems more reasonable and safer to take the well-trodden path than to let God lead you on an unfamiliar path. No wonder it is written in Isaiah 55:8-9: *"For My thoughts are not your thoughts, neither are your ways My ways. As the heavens are higher than the earth, so are My ways higher than your ways and My thoughts than your thoughts."* I rejoiced with her that she had heard God correctly and that she had been obedient to Him even though in the natural, the situation that she was facing seemed impossible to be changed in her favor.

7. Wanting to hear what you want to hear

I have met people who not only go around collecting prophetic words but also want the prophetic word to agree with what they want to happen in their lives. For example, there was a lady who wanted a certain relationship to have a particular outcome. So, when the prophetic word that she received was different from the one that she wanted to hear, she just ignored it. She keeps seeking a prophetic word that agrees with what she wants to hear.

This is very dangerous because sometimes an immature prophetic person may pick up on your desires in the spiritual realm and start to prophesy out your desires when it is not God's word to you. However, since it's what you want to hear, you will be very happy to receive this type of prophetic word, even though it is not from God. If things take a bad turn, it is likely that you will blame God. In the area of relationships, many emotionally involved people will claim that they have prayed about it and that the person is God's choice for them, even though everyone else thinks otherwise. I have met many Christians who have already made up their mind to marry someone with whom they are unequally yoked. They may even claim that God has asked them to marry that non-Christian, so that the person may later become a Christian through them.

Another example was when both my husband and I wanted to start a furniture business ten years ago. There were people who advised us not to do so, but we had already basically decided that we wanted to start the business. We ignored the advice completely and called these people "dream stealers." In hindsight, I realized that our "good" idea was not a "God" idea. I paid a heavy price for not learning early in my Christian journey that one of the hindrances to hearing God's voice is wanting to hear what I wanted to hear. I frequently use this valuable lesson I have learned to warn the people that I teach so that they won't make the same mistake that I made.

8. When you are paralyzed by fear

An example in the Bible of fear drowning out the truth can be found when Elijah was running for his life from Jezebel. He was full of fear and said to God in 1 Kings 19:10, 14: *"They have killed God's prophets with the sword, and I am the only one left."* The truth was that the false prophets were the ones who were killed by Elijah. The events Elijah recounted to God were the opposite of what had actually happened. Elijah was mistaken because fear for his life blurred his perception and he was not remembering things clearly. He was telling God what he saw through the eyes of fear. He didn't see the situation truthfully and clearly because he was overwhelmed with fear. Therefore, when it comes to hearing God's voice, if you are afraid or if you are moving in fear, you must be aware that fear can blur your perception of the truth even when God is speaking to you.

9. Feeling of frustration

Another hindrance you might face is if you are "frustrated" or if you "try too hard" to hear His voice.

In his book, *Stepping into the Prophetic,* Peter Christensen wrote:

> *One of the hardest times to hear the voice of the Lord is when we are frustrated. This often comes as a result of allowing problems to take root in our thinking patterns. The only way to rectify this is through casting down every thought and imagination that is contrary to the nature of Christ (2 Corinthians 10:5). By doing this we are stilling our minds from being overactive and opening up our heart to receive from the Holy Spirit. In Jeremiah 15:16, it reads: 'Your words were found, and I ate them, and your word was to me the joy and rejoicing of my heart.' Here Jeremiah expresses his excitement*

and joy over discovering the word of the Lord. Prior to this, he was frustrated and wanted to quit the ministry.

In the course of my teaching, I have seen many Christians trying very hard but still not able to hear God's voice. This has resulted in them ending up feeling frustrated and sometimes annoyed with themselves. They may also feel envious of those who can hear His voice easily. God is no respecter of persons, and He will definitely let you hear His voice. You only need to still your spirit before Him, realizing you do not need to rely on your own effort, but on His love for you. Frustration comes when you feel you have tried so hard but there is no evidence that you've heard God's voice. As you come to our heavenly Father with the faith of a child, you can be sure He will not in any way ignore you or let you remain in your frustration. He will certainly open all your spiritual senses so that you can hear Him.

10. Lack of obedience

Learning to hear God's voice is not difficult but obeying what He tells us to do is the challenge for most of us. I have seen some Christians who go around collecting prophecy after prophecy. Whenever they hear a prophet is in town, they will be found in the meeting. Sadly, they fail to realize that nearly every prophetic word that is received regarding anointing, ministry, or moving in the power of the Holy Spirit has prerequisites that need to be obeyed before they can see the fulfillment of the prophetic word.

The prerequisite to obey the Lord is part of your preparation or part of the breaking, purifying, and molding process. You will find that if you do not obey the voice of God, over time you will begin to become dull in your hearing. Many times, you may not like or agree with what the heavenly Father is showing you. So, you pout, you argue, and then you choose to completely ignore what He has said. You fail to realize that the hearing part is over, and you have already heard and now it is a matter of obedience. One thing that hinders you from hearing God's voice is when you try to move on without first obeying. You may also find that if you resist God in one area of your life, then you will also most likely resist Him in the other areas that He is shining His light on. Often, He gives you a prophetic word to test your heart and your obedience. He is an ever-gracious Father who wants you to willingly surrender your life to Him so that He can mold you to be His light and salt in this world.

11. The feeling of despair and discouragement

When you are in despair or feeling discouraged, you may find it very difficult to hear God's voice because everything that you perceive or see is dark, bleak, and hopeless. Sometimes you may be so discouraged that when God sends a person to give you an encouraging prophetic word, you will reject it even though it is accurate. Due to the discouragement and despair, you have hardened your heart and therefore won't believe any prophetic word that is given to you. An example of how discouragement can cause you to not listen to God is recorded in Exodus 6:1-8 when Moses told the Israelites that God would deliver them from the bondage of the Pharaoh and would bring them to the land He had sworn to Abraham, Isaac, and Jacob for their possession. However, in Exodus 6:9 it is written, *"Moses reported this to the Israelites, but they did not listen to him because of their discouragement and harsh labor"* (emphasis mine).

When you feel discouraged, it is easier for you to wallow in the "poor me" mentality than to believe what God says, either directly to you or through a prophetic word.

In their book, *God Encounters,* James and Michal Ann Goll wrote:

> *After suffering a major blow, we sometimes feel 'knocked out of adjustment' and in need of heavy-duty maintenance. Some of us may require a 'lube' job or a 'timing' adjustment, while others need a major overhaul of internal working parts.*

In such times, it is so important to have the body of Christ standing and interceding with you, as you're not in a position to pray, nor feel inclined to do so. You may not even have the spiritual energy to pray for yourself. You feel "flat" and may even reach the point of just giving up. In such instances, you are in no frame of mind to hear His voice concerning the situation you are facing. Therefore, it is easy for you to begin to believe the lie from the enemy that you have done something wrong and so you have become "unworthy" and "too impure and guilty" to hear His voice. The more you believe this lie, the more you will feel discouraged and this may even lead you to sink slowly into depression. However, God in His mercy and love will impress upon someone to intercede for you so that you can overcome this feeling of despair and discouragement. During such times, you will really appreciate intercessors and loved ones who stand by you when you are going through the "dark valley" experience. I encourage you to be the one who stands by someone who is going through such discouragement and despair. This is because one day when you yourself go through such a "dark valley" experience, you will be so thankful that someone stood alongside you in intercession.

12. When your eyes and ear gates are not cleansed

There may be some people whose mind and imagination are always thinking of sexual and impure thoughts and this will hinder them from hearing God's voice. They may have previously submitted their "eye-gate" to pornography and this has caused Satan to have a foothold in their mind and imagination.

Mark Virkler in his book, *Hearing God Through Biblical Meditation*, wrote:

"Your imagination is a canvas that was designed to be painted upon by the brushstrokes of heaven."

So, does this mean if your imagination is filled with sexual and impure thoughts that you have no hope of ever hearing God's voice? I have good news for you—God in His mercy and love for you has given you a way to hear His voice even when you are in such a state of mind. First of all, you must realize that the source of sexual and impure images is from the devil. You must bind and break and renounce the spirit of pornography or lust. After that, if any of the sexual images come into your imagination again, you must resist it and command it to go in Jesus' name. You have the authority to command every thought to be held in captivity to the mind of Christ. God's thoughts will then become your thoughts if you focus on Him.

Kenneth McDonald in his book, *Prophetic Seminar Handbook,* wrote:

> *When you have a thought that is impure, then say 'No, I take that thought captive in Jesus' name. Not today!' Thoughts are like birds that fly overhead. We cannot stop them from flying over our heads, but we can stop them from lighting in our trees.*

In Patricia King's book, *Ears to Hear,* she wrote about cleansing the "ear gates" from defiling influences so that this will help you hear clearly the voice of the Lord:

> *The world is full of communication that is disturbing to our spirits. If we fill our hearts and minds with things that are contrary to God's word, then we can be blocked from hearing the true voice of God. What we listen to enters our soul. Our minds and beliefs are indeed influenced by what we hear. Invite the Lord to cleanse your ear gate from any and all defiling words and thoughts that are contrary to the Word of God. You simply need to ask Him, and He will.*

13. Having a wrong mindset or wrong theology

The dictionary defines "mindset" as "a fixed mental attitude, habit or disposition that pre-determines a person's responses to and interpretations of situations." A mindset is when you have already made up your mind about how certain things will happen, or what God needs to say to you, or what you want Him to do, etc. It is very similar to an opinion, except most of the time, a mindset has a certain amount of blindness. It is the way that you see things, and this can lead you to be blind to anything other than your perspective. You do not even know that you are blinded by this mindset. When God tries to say something about it to you, you may find yourself thinking that it doesn't make sense to you and so you just dismiss what He says. You may have a certain mindset about the theology of the prophetic or how God should speak to you and this can hinder you from hearing His voice.

Lyn Packer, in her book, *Releasing Heaven on Earth* wrote:

> *Sometimes our experiences and our emotions can shout louder than what the Scripture speaks, and because of that, we can sometimes begin to form a new theology, which we then believe, embrace and live out of. We begin to justify our position with statements like, 'Well Scripture doesn't really mean that,' or 'God doesn't want to heal everyone,' or 'It's not God's time' etc., and before we know it we have a theology that is quite different from what Scripture says. If we're really honest, most of us live out of our tweaked theology in some areas more than we live out of what Scripture actually does say.*

14. Having pride in your life

Pride is the attitude that declares, "I know what is best for me and I choose to whom I will listen." It's having the "I know it all" or "I have arrived and there is nothing else I can learn from anyone" attitude. Pride also tells you your future is in your own hands, so it is entirely up to your effort to make yourself successful and it has nothing to do with God or hearing His voice.

Pride can also keep you from being open to the possibility that God might want to say something to you about your situation. Pride tells you that you only need Him when you have problems and if you can handle your problems yourself, then you do not really need to hear from Him. You may think that if and when you cannot solve your problems, then and only then will you need to ask Him about His thoughts on the situation you are facing.

This will result in an unteachable attitude towards God. It may also result in you not repenting or taking responsibility for any wrongdoing. The Bible says in James 4:6 that *"God resists the proud but gives grace to the humble."*

When you are humble, you are always seeking God as you want to hear from Him regarding every situation that you are facing. When you are prideful, you do not think that you need to ask Him because you already know what to do, so why bother to ask Him? Many times, God may send warning signs to avert disaster in a prideful person's life, but if this person is controlled by pride, they may be unable or unwilling to recognize His voice. The scary part is that a prideful Christian may have already stopped hearing the voice of God in his life but may not even realize that he is already missing that connection with Him.

In 2 Chronicles 26: 4-5, we read, *"King Uzziah sought the Lord during the days of Zechariah, who instructed him in the fear of God."* As long as King Uzziah sought God, he became prosperous and successful (2 Chronicles 26:5). Unfortunately, after Zechariah died, Uzziah started thinking he was not accountable to anyone. He became proud and he angrily rejected the counsel of eighty-one godly priests who had told him to get out of the sanctuary (2 Chronicles 26:18). Instead of heeding their warning, he became very angry and God struck him with leprosy. King Uzziah was a leper until the day of his death.

Sometimes, you may hear a prophetic word that shines a light on the pride in your life. How you respond to this type of prophetic word is important. If your pride takes over, instead of taking the opportunity to ask God for forgiveness and humble yourself, you may instead get angry with the person giving the prophetic word. You may feel no one has the right to correct you. In such an instance, your heart can become more hardened and calloused until you cannot hear God's voice anymore, either directly from Him, or through a prophetic word.

15. Depending on others to hear God for you

This is very common among people who know a bit about the value of a prophetic word but are not willing to invest their time to hear God for themselves. They want to take the shortcut of asking someone else to seek a prophetic word for them. This is by no means new to God, as even in the Old Testament God wanted to speak to the Israelites directly, but they were afraid of Him, so they asked Moses to listen to all that the Lord said and then tell them so that they could obey (Deuteronomy 5:27). Because of Jesus' death on the cross, He has reconciled you to God, so you can now come boldly before God. Therefore, you do not need to fear Him like the Israelites did when God appeared to them in the form of thunder and fire. You can now *"come boldly to Mount Zion, to the city of the living God, the heavenly Jerusalem, and to myriads of angels, to the general assembly… and to the spirit of righteous men made perfect"* (Hebrews 12:22-23).

16. When you expect God to speak to you in the way you expect or on your terms or in your time frame

You may be waiting for something dramatic or a burning bush experience when God speaks to you. This can hinder you from hearing God's voice when He uses ordinary day-to-day things to speak to you. When you hear that God speaks to your friends in a particular way, you may also expect Him to speak to you in the same way. If He uses a different way to speak to you, you may be unable to discern His voice. Many times, when you speak to Him, you may also expect Him to speak and respond to you within your timeframe (which is not God's timeframe). If you do not hear Him within the expected timeframe, you may then decide that He does not want to speak to you at all.

17. When you feel complacent

According to Webster Dictionary, "complacency" is described as "self-satisfaction, especially when accompanied by unawareness of actual dangers or deficiencies; a feeling of being satisfied with how things are and not wanting to try to make them better."

Complacency may limit your ability to have the motivation to bring about a change in your life and this, in turn, prevents you from working out the fullness of your destiny. Complacency says, "Do nothing." The attitude of complacency is like what is described in Zephaniah 1:12: *"At that time I will search Jerusalem with lamps, and I will punish the men who are complacent, those who say in their hearts, 'The Lord will not do good, nor will He do ill.'"*

You may be in this state of complacency and cannot be bothered to pursue God or wait patiently for Him to speak. You may feel it is not important, urgent, or worthwhile enough for you to find time to speak to Him or wait for Him to speak to you. Complacency can clog your ears to hear His voice according to what Lana Vawser wrote in her book, *Desperately Deeper*:

> *The greatest clogs in today's church is complacency. Complacency says, 'I am comfortable where I am, and I choose to remain in this place. I am not desperate enough to sacrifice my comfort in order to grow.' If we find ourselves in a place of complacency, it is because we are comfortable where we are and not very hungry. Seeing more of who Jesus Christ is, hearing His voice and seeing His heart shatters all complacency because we cannot live in a dynamic relationship with Jesus Christ without being changed.*

18. When you have experienced disappointment with God

Disappointment with God is more common and a bigger hindrance than you might realize. In the natural, if you are disappointed with someone, you feel hurt because that person did not do what you thought they should do. In such an instance, you might close your heart to that person and even when you see them, there is a distance between you. Whatever this person says, you are unable to receive, or you may feel cynical whenever that person speaks. You feel distrustful of that person as you've been hurt by that person before.

In the spiritual sense, you may have been disappointed with God because you prayed and sought God over something important in your life, but nothing has happened. This could be healing for someone and that person has not been healed. Subsequently, when God speaks to you about healing, you may "turn off," not only in the area of healing but also in any other areas that God may speak to you about. You feel hurt and rejected, and you blame God for not answering your prayers and for not being fair to you. This disappointment with God may hinder you from hearing His voice.

When you are disappointed with God, most of the time, there is grief and pain associated with it. You feel you cannot trust God anymore and you do not believe anything He says to you. I have come across many people who have been disappointed when prophetic words that were spoken over their lives did not come to pass. However, many times, they fail to ask God about the timing or the prerequisites concerning the prophetic word that they received. When things do not turn out the way they think it should, they become angry and disappointed with God. Therefore, when someone gives them a prophetic word, they will view the person giving the prophetic word as a scammer and so they do not believe the prophetic word at all, even though the prophetic word is true and accurate.

19. When you have unresolved offenses or grief

Unresolved offenses with someone can also cause you to lose your peace. When your heart is in turmoil, this can drown out God's gentle voice when He speaks to you. When you are offended by what someone did to you, you begin to hold a grudge. Inevitably, all your mind can think about is the offense, even when you try to pray or hear God's voice. The grief and offense crowd everything you think about and you are not in any state of mind to hear His voice due to this blockage. You need the body of Christ to help you to get out of this state of mind by interceding for you so that you can be whole again to hear His voice.

You may have unresolved grief due to the loss of loved ones or the loss of health or finances. You may not be able to understand why you need to go through these difficult situations even though you are serving God and have prayed earnestly for God to intervene. As a result, when God speaks to you regarding healing, health, or finance, you may be unable to receive what God says as you are still grieving over what happened in your life. This is especially true when you have prayed for the healing of your loved ones and they have not been healed and may have even passed away, in spite of many prophetic words saying that your loved ones would be healed.

On this note, I would like to share about my brother, Charles, who went to be with the Lord four years ago. When I was praying for his healing, I was sure God showed me that he would be healed and that he would go to different churches to share his testimony. When he passed away, my faith in my ability to hear God's voice accurately was shipwrecked. I found it very difficult to reconcile the prophetic word with what actually happened. I began to doubt when God spoke His heart to me about other people. I was in this place of doubt and grief until one day, my niece, Liz, shared that she'd had a dream about her dad. In the dream, she asked her dad why he had to go so soon. In the dream, her dad said, *"I was so tired, you see."* My brother was not able to sleep and eat properly for the last six to eight months before he passed away. Liz felt sad that her dad had been so tired, and she couldn't do anything to help. However, after the dream, she understood that her dad wanted to go home to be with the Lord. She was thankful that her dad was released from the pain that he had suffered for so long.

In his book, *Prophetic Warfare,* Les D. Crause gave this valuable insight:

> *And if you are praying for somebody who is dying, and in their heart, they have made up their mind they are sick of this world and they want to go and be with the Lord, give them a break. They want to go. You cannot overrule their will. The Lord does not overrule our will. Satan is the one who overrules our will.*

May this give some comfort to those who feel angry or disappointed with God because they felt that God did not answer their prayer regarding the healing of their loved ones.

20. When you have feelings of bitterness

Bitterness is the agony you feel as a result of blaming God, or someone else for the work of Satan, sin or self. When you hold on to hurt, resentment, or a grudge, then you're not going to be able to hear God, because your heart is hardened. It has grown cold and made you defensive, even to God's love. A bitter spirit sees God as unapproachable and unavailable. An example is Job who in the midst of his anger, cried out in Job 23:2-4, *"Even today my complaint is bitter; his hand is heavy in spite of my groaning. If only I knew where to find him if only, I could go to his dwelling. I would state my case before him and fill my mouth with arguments."* In essence, Job is implying that he wished God was available so he could argue his case. When you feel bitterness in your heart, you may pray but you actually feel that God is distant and is not listening to you. You may give up praying as you may not be in the frame of mind to hear Him when He speaks.

The Good News

The good news is that although you may experience many hindrances to hearing God's voice, He wants to help you overcome all these hindrances if you let Him. God is loving, merciful, and kind. He will help you overcome all these hindrances, and nothing can stop Him from letting you hear Him if you call out to Him. Do you know that even at the eleventh hour, on the death bed, God is still speaking to bring the dying person into His Kingdom? Nothing can separate you from His love, and He will be relentless in wooing you. Open your heart to Him and you will never be the same again. You must remember that though hearing from God is important, this should not be your ultimate goal. Instead, your main goal should be to become a spiritually mature person who desires a closer relationship with God, rather than just to hear His voice to get an answer for what you are seeking. When you have an intimate relationship with God, you will be able to correctly hear what God has to say to you and more importantly, to know what is in His heart.

In Jim Goll's book, *The Seer*, he warned:

> *Along with our passionate seeking, we must learn how to balance between the objective and, the subjective experience. An objective experience is not determined by impressions, feelings, inner vision or voices but is based upon convictions concerning God's character—His faithfulness to keep His promises. A subjective experience, on the other hand, is the cry of the soul for a clearer awareness of God; the passionate desire for a distinct hearing of His voice. Whatever we do, we must maintain our balance between the subjective and the objective. We must not become so fixated on the prophetic or visionary revelation that we throw away the Bible. Let us keep our objectivity. The revelatory word is not a competitor with the written Word, but a complement to it, and always subordinate to it. The written*

Word of God is the unwavering standard by which all revelatory word must be measured.

Remember that you may be looking for answers, but your heavenly Father is looking for intimacy; this should be your goal when you are learning to hear His voice. Hearing His voice will be the natural by-product that is born out of the intimate relationship with your heavenly Father. Indeed, Jesus said in John 15:5 that *"No longer do I call you slaves, for the slave does not know what his master is doing, but I have called you friends, for all things that I have heard from My Father, I have made known to you."* When you have this intimate relationship, then all the things Jesus hears will be made known to you.

Prayer

Dear heavenly Father, I thank You that You love me so much that if I allow You to help me, there is nothing that can hinder me from hearing Your voice. Please show me the hindrances that are stopping me from hearing your voice. Help me to yield to You so that these hindrances can be removed. I want nothing to prevent me from hearing Your voice. Forgive me for trying to hear Your voice so that I can get answers from You when You are instead longing for intimacy with me. Help me to have this as my goal for I know that when I have an intimate relationship with You, hearing Your voice will just be a natural by-product of that, so I do not need to struggle or strive. In Jesus' name. Amen.

Activation exercises

1. Holy Spirit, can you please show me/tell me one hindrance I have that is preventing me from hearing my heavenly Father's voice?

2. Holy Spirit, can you please show me/tell me what I must do to remove this hindrance?

3. Holy Spirit, can you please show me/tell me any other hindrances that are not mentioned above that may be preventing me from hearing the heavenly Father's voice? Please show me/tell me what I must do in order to remove these hindrances?

SUMMARY

Though the list of hindrances you may face when wanting to hear God's voice seems long, you must remember God is able to help you to overcome all of these if you will allow Him to do so. In the final analysis, you must remember that ultimately hearing His voice is the by-product born of an intimate relationship with Him. You no longer need to struggle or strive to hear His voice when you have this intimate relationship with Him. Indeed, Jesus said in John 15:5 that *"No longer do I call you slaves, for the slave does not know what his master is doing, but I have called you friends, for all things that I have heard from My Father, I have made known to you."* When you have this intimate relationship with

Him, then all the things Jesus hears will be made known to you. Indeed, as His sheep, you will be able to hear His voice in every area of your life.

CONCLUSION

We have come to the end of this book where you have learned step-by-step how to hear God's voice. I have enjoyed sharing what I have learned with you. You can stand on my shoulders and go higher and deeper and faster than I have ever been before. I did not have any actual face-to-face mentors to help me along the way. I would love for you to learn in a group setting how to hear His voice. If you are interested to learn more about how to hear God's voice, feel free to send a message to rindahoauthor@gmail.com. I would love to hear from you.

If you are reading this book and you do not know this God whom I've spoken about and you would like to know more, I would love to connect with you. You can email your questions to rindahoauthor@gmail.com. I would love to help you to take the step of asking Jesus into your heart so that you can start this amazing journey of hearing His voice. Alternatively, you can pray this prayer below:

"Dear God, I do not know You, but it seems that You know me and created me according to what I have read in this book. Can You please show me in a tangible way that You hear me and that You want to connect with me? I am told that if I admit my sin and believe that Jesus died for my sins and ask You to forgive me, then I will become

Your child. Jesus, I admit that I am a sinner and that You died on the cross for my sins. Please forgive my sins. I ask You to come into my heart. Thank You, Jesus, that I am now a child of God. I believe that now I can have this intimate relationship with You and that You will guide me and direct me so that I can fulfill my destiny on this earth. In Jesus' name. Amen."

THANK YOU

Thank you for reading this book. I pray that you have been blessed and that you are ready to continue to hear God's voice in every area of your life. I would like to bless you with a short ebook, *10 Questions You May Have About Hearing God's Voice*. These are additional questions not covered in the book, but possibly questions that you have. If you are interested in getting this short ebook, you can get it here: https://www.subscribepage.com/j7k6m5_copy

I also do periodic webinars. You can stay informed about upcoming webinars and my mentoring group for those who would like to go deeper and higher in learning to God's voice by following this link: https://landing.mailerlite.com/webforms/landing/l7n6j3

If this book has blessed you and you have found it useful, I'd be very grateful if you'd post an honest review. Your review will encourage others to go on their personal journey to hear God's voice as well. Your review will also help me to get the message to as many people as possible, so that they too can learn to hear God's voice and fulfill the destiny that God has for them.

If you would like to leave a review, then all you need to do is go to the review section on the book's Amazon page. You'll see a big button that says "Write a customer review." Click that and you're good to go!

TESTIMONIES FROM CHRISTIANS WHO HAVE LEARNED TO HEAR GOD'S VOICE

I have included testimonies from people who have attended my teaching and mentoring sessions that I have conducted. These are their responses to "What has happened in your spiritual life since learning to hear His voice? How has learning to hear God's voice changed your Christian walk?" I have also included testimonies from other Christians who shared how hearing God's voice has helped them in their Christian walk.

"As a result of learning to hear God's voice, I now have a deeper and more enriching relationship with God. My prayer life has improved tremendously as I am feeling God's presence daily and it is no longer a monologue of waiting. I strongly recommend learning this basic skill if you are a Christian. This experience will change your intimacy with God."

—**Mervyn Ch'ng**

"'What is God's plan for my life?' Have you asked that question before? Why not ask God Himself what is His plans for you? I have learned that hearing from Him is not a special once-in-awhile event, but it is the time spent daily in His presence, dialoguing with a Father who loves me. He is eager and willing to speak; it is only up to us to seek His presence. I have learned in simple, easy-to-understand steps to be in tune with His voice and to listen to the heart of the Father. I believe this is an essential ability that every Christian should have."

—**Gerard Chin**

"I have learned that hearing from God is very easy and it just requires me to speak out in faith and not doubt the first thing that comes to my mind. I just need to discern that the words I speak out are always encouraging and not condemning words as our God is a good God. I can use my five senses to discern whether what I heard was from God. I discovered that my strength lies in hearing and as I asked God, 'What can I do for you, Lord?' I was able to discern God saying to me, 'Son, go in My strength.' I knew that the Lord was reminding me, that I cannot win souls for the Lord based on my experience or my own strength, but I have to be sensitive to His spirit and just by faith to take God's hand and allow Him to lead me to be His Treasure Hunter. God is asking me to be strong and courageous for Him and He will take me on an exciting journey of winning souls for His kingdom. I was amazed that God can say that to me and at the same time felt humbled and confident again in my spirit."

—**Calvin Lim**

"Before I learned how to hear God's voice, I thought that I had to fulfill certain spiritual criteria such as being a leader in the church or to read the bible every day, in order to hear his voice. I always admired and envied people who saw visions or heard God speaking to them. I felt discouraged and wondered why I couldn't be like them. Lots of negative thoughts started to come into my mind. After learning to hear

God's voice, I realized that it is actually an image or word that comes first into our mind when we ask God to reveal something to us. I was really excited when God started to download a word or a vision to me for other people and I just kept writing as I was being led by the spirit. When I first took the step of faith to give a prophetic word to two of my connect group members, they told me that the word from God ministered to their current situations which I was actually unaware of. I thanked God and felt very encouraged that God can use me to bless his people. It has always been my heart's desire to hear God's voice and to encourage people whom He sends into my life. I am really thankful and excited as I know that my spiritual journey will never be the same again."

—**Lee H**

"I am amazed at how easy it is to hear God's voice. I write every day, especially during my prayer time in the morning when He speaks to me. Having a conversation and hearing from Him has become a daily part of my life."

—**Pat Lim**

"When I was learning how to hear God's voice, I was quite new to the Holy Spirit and was just trying to figure out what people meant by asking the Lord for direction and confirmation. All I could receive was warmth or peace when praying. To my astonishment, I started to see a vision and hear God's voice to a level beyond my imagination. I could never imagine reaching this level within such a short time of less than a year. Now not only could I hear and communicate with God for myself, but I could also receive words of knowledge for people during our prayer sessions. I started participating in a healing and prayer ministry and found it to be really rewarding, knowing that the Lord is using me as a vessel to assist and support His people. I am still dumbfounded that people are coming to me for prayers and healing. It is surreal. I have never envisaged myself, a layperson, doing that. The ability to feel and share God's presence among people is really amazing."

—**Mary Lim**

"I did not know and realize how basic and easy it is to access God's voice until I had been taught. Eyes opening and absolutely essential!"

—**Olivia Lee**

"What really impacted me and changed my perspective on prayer and hearing from God, was the simple fact that God desires to speak to us, and we as His children can hear His voice. There was no requirement or technicalities to hearing from God. I've also learned to discern God's voice, my voice, and the voice of the enemy. This has helped me capture negative thoughts about myself or certain situations and people and tune in to God's voice instead."

—**Ashley Keasberry**

"When I was learning to hear God's voice, I had doubts and skepticism of the prophetic gift being exclusive and its effectiveness. I learned that all of us have the gift to hear God's voice through any or all of our five senses. I also grew in confidence in being able to release His word to someone else. Discovering and developing this gift of prophecy has edified and encouraged us immensely and given us renewed purpose in our spiritual walk. We have continually exercised our gift, each time, edifying the individual receiving the word, as well as reaffirming God's presence in our lives."

—**Augustine and Susan Teow**

"My youngest daughter was about to finish her master's degree in July 2016. At the beginning of that year, she started to worry that there were not many employment opportunities for her course. She discussed with me whether she had chosen the right course. I told her to keep on going and I will keep her in prayer since she would complete her course in six months' time. I committed her concerns in prayer. One day while praying, God showed me a vision of many antique lamps that were lighting a dark tunnel. God gave me the interpretation that my daughter's future and the pathway that she is taking will be lit up. Psalm 119:105 came to my thoughts: *'Your word is a lamp for my feet and a light to my path.'* Later that day, when I went shopping, I saw exactly the same lamp that I saw in my vision. In the next few days, when I went into another antique shop, I saw the same type of lamp that I saw in my vision again. A few days later, when I went shopping, for the third time, I saw the same type of antique lamp again. It was as if God was confirming to me that He will be a lamp for my daughter's feet and a light for her path. I could not wait to share the good news with my daughter so that she wouldn't worry about her future. In March 2016, even before my daughter had completed her course, she was offered a fellowship to pursue her Ph.D. in the United Kingdom. The fellowship was founded by the European Union. As soon as she finished her master's degree, she started on her Ph.D. I thank God that because I have learned to hear His voice, I could interpret the vision which He used to assure me of His guidance upon my daughter's life."

—**Mary Yap**

"Truly Rinda's teaching leads me to a whole new next level with God. I deeply realized that His desire is to love me more and guide me each step according to His will. His love for me is even more than I longed for Him. He is such a loving, tender, gracious God full of mercy, and His profound love overwhelmed me each time when I listen to Him. Whenever we have a problem, we tend to go to other people for advice, direction, and guidance and even ask them to seek answers from God on our behalf. However, Rinda's teaching taught me that I can go directly to Him and ask Him for His intimate guidance and to dwell in His immense love and presence. That's the very place we all ever want to be and ever should be. This inordinate and unthinkable blessings of hearing from our Creator will surely take anyone to a whole different world of deeper intimacy with our amazing Sovereign God."

—**Julie**

"Learning to hear God's voice has absolutely led me to another level of my faith in God and honestly, my walk with God has become so much easier as I learned to be obedient to what He has asked me to do. I discovered that I can utilize my spiritual senses and my spiritual gifts to minister to other people. Learning to hear God's voice has helped me to build an intimate relationship with God and I am able to continue my Christian journey without turning away from Him as I used to do so before I learned to hear His voice."

—**Sujeong Choi**

"I had no idea how easy it was to hear God's voice. I had not realized God was already talking to me, giving me visions and words. The teaching gave me the hands-on exercise and the prayer to pray before writing down what God said to me. This was done in a way that opened all of my spiritual senses. Since attending the teaching, I have put what I've learned into practice. One example is one day while I was worshipping at our connect group, I had a vision of a bridge and the word 'connect' came to me. I wasn't going to say anything, but the

Holy Spirit continued to prompt me. I shared the vision and the word that God has given me with the group and shared that I felt that God was encouraging us to connect to Him through the worship."

—**Katherine Hayes**

"We both thoroughly enjoyed the teaching which was spoken to us all in love and made hearing the voices of God seem so easy and natural. It was really encouraging to know that God is talking to us all the time. We just need to trust His Voice more and act on it. The exercises that were given to practice listening were very helpful and gave us confidence that we were actually hearing from our heavenly Father. We feel that since doing the course our spiritual antennas are much more alert and tuned towards God and that the gentle thoughts and impressions that we get are most likely from God. We are learning to better discern His voice. During the training, we were encouraged to talk to God and ask Him questions about what He is saying to us. We also feel more confident in stepping out to give encouraging words to people that God lays on our hearts."

—**Graham and Dianne Storey**

"I am truly so blessed to have attended the training session, as my quiet time has never been better. I didn't realize that God had already been speaking to me on most occasions because I always felt that I was not worthy of Him. Upon learning about how to hear God's voice, I prayed and submitted myself to the Holy Spirit to open all my spiritual senses so that I can understand what God is saying. Topics were discussed clearly and were to the point. The examples and activation exercise helped me in understanding how to hear God's voice."

—**Beh Maglunog**

"The teaching has helped me in this area of hearing God's voice. I am now more aware of His voice, His prompting and also His guidance. Just the other day, when I was at the evening prayer team, I sensed that God wanted me to pray for the spirit of religion to be broken. So, I prayed along that line to declare that the spirit of religion to be broken. I have learned that our relationship with God is an intimate relationship like that of a Father with His sons/daughters. Thank you for showing and teaching us how to open our spiritual senses to see, hear, and sense what our heavenly Father wants to tell us."

—**Steven Ngoo**

"After the teaching, I find myself praising our heavenly Father more frequently in my day-to-day chores and being more sensitive to His presence. I just feel like I'm being nudged to keep glorifying Him, whether things are bad or good at the time."

—**Lianti**

"Thank you for your wonderful teaching on how to hear the voice of God. Indeed, this has been my desire for a while to find out how to really hear from God and how to have a dialogue with Him. Through the teaching, I have learned that God can communicate with us in so many ways, it's just that we never really realized it. I am now more aware and sensitive to His voice and more in tune to receive messages from Him. Now my walk with Christ is even closer and deeper as I rely more on the Holy Spirit than my own strength in many situations."

—**Lynn Ngoo**

"When I was pregnant with my daughter Calvary, I was extremely sick and landed myself twice in the hospital attached to a drip for dehydration. In a dream, I was holding a baby in my arms and it had been pierced by many arrows. I didn't know what to do, so in my dream, I waited for my husband, Matt to come back home. We decided to pull the arrows from her. I distinctly remember pulling what appeared to be a stick from in between her pointer finger and thumb and her flesh literally disintegrated. I was very angry, and I instantly knew this was the work of the enemy. I saw a battlefield in my mind where the enemy line was within a distance to where I was and I planned to march up to the enemy line and unleash by saying, 'Do you even know who I am? Do you know that I am a daughter of the Most High God? I have authority over you—what right and how DARE you attack me.' Instantly, I knew it was a trap. I saw that if I went over there and exposed my anger, I would be exposing myself to more attacks. I heard the words so very clearly. 'It's going to be okay. *Just stand on my Word.*' I don't know if the voice was audible or just in my spirit, but it was so quiet and calm. Whenever I go through situations I don't understand, I hear those words so clearly: 'Just stand on my Word.' This is a daily discipline that sometimes I do well at and quite frankly, some days I fail. As humans, we are very fragile and are quick to forget, but His Word is my instruction manual to life. I have many instances where God has spoken to me regarding ministry and my children. It is a voice that is very, very different to my own inner voice. When I have a human idea, it comes up in my spirit as a question, whereas when God speaks to me, it's very matter of fact. There is no question in it. I have learned to recognize the difference between my voice and His voice."

—Sofia Gibbons

"In mid- 2018, I wanted to pursue a career in the army. However, even after training very hard and trying for many years, I could not pass the medical requirements. I even resigned from a teaching position in the bid to fulfill this dream. Before the last tryout, I asked God to take away this desire if this was not for me. After receiving the last rejection letter, the desire to be in the armed forces was indeed diminished, though I didn't know what else God had in store for me.

During that time, I decided to take a small break and go on holiday. When I came back after a few months, I couldn't find a job for a few months. I applied for as many teaching positions as I could, but for some strange reasons, when I called up to check on the progress of my application, they informed me that they had misplaced it. I was feeling disheartened. During that time, I took a casual position. During that time, God was shining this light on my prideful, egoistic and arrogant attitude while I was working there. He used that season to teach me to be patient, humble and gracious to others. As I started to focus less on myself and more on God, He used two messages to speak into my life. That week, I asked God for forgiveness and re-surrendered my life to Him and prayed that the Holy Spirit will once again lead me towards God's plan.

That same week, I suddenly received three job offers. This was indeed a miracle as previously my applications were either misplaced or rejected. I sought the Lord on which offer I should accept. He gave me the answer that He will never short change me and He reminded me not to chase after money and to depend on Him. I felt led to accept the lower salary position, but I wanted God to confirm whether I had made the right decision. He is so gracious that He gave me three signs. The first sign was prior to the commencement of my interview at the Christian school when my interviewers started with a prayer. I felt the spiritual atmosphere changed in that room and I felt tremendous peace. Secondly, the timing of the job offer came through my friend who informed me that her school might have an opening. This came just as I was thinking of accepting the higher paying job. I have worked as a casual in that school four years ago. I decided to contact the person who was the relief co-ordinator when I was working there, but it turned out that he is now the principal. He immediately offered me a part-time position. The third sign was that my future direct supervisor is a very good Christian teacher and I would be learning how to be a good Christian teacher from her. With these three signs, I accepted the lower salary part-time position, even though I will be getting $30,000 less than the other two job offers.

As soon as I signed the contract, the school also offered me a higher paying scale and also increased my hours as well as giving me a new laptop. On top of that, before I actually started work in the school, I was miraculously made full time and was back paid for 4 weeks of holidays, even though I have not even started working in the school yet. Indeed, God's blessings just keep on pouring in and He indeed He is able to do exceedingly abundantly above what we ask or think. I am now working full time in a school that is only one minute's drive from my home. I have great colleagues and also have many opportunities to grow professionally. In retrospective, the rejection and closed door that I have encountered has, in the end, led me to this massive blessing. God is indeed always on time and has good and perfect gifts in store for all of us."

—**Samantha C**

"I have heard God's voice in many different ways. Often it is like that still, small whisper that speaks straight into my soul. Usually, I feel a prompting from the Holy Spirit—a sense or feeling I guess you could say. As I ask God to speak, there is where I hear His Voice. Recently, when praying about what 2019 would look like for me and my family, I had a feeling that we would move to a new house this year. Again, it was a sense, a feeling not from my own thoughts, but from God. God has also spoken to me through clear visions. Once as I lay on my bed waiting to fall asleep, the presence of God fell upon my body. I felt pinned to my bed. There God showed me a vision of a future season I was about to enter, and He showed me the details of how it was going to happen. It was vivid and tangible."

—**Taryn Hamilton**

PLEASE SHARE

If you enjoyed this book and found some benefit in reading this, I'd like to hear from you and hope that you could take some time to post an honest review on Amazon.

Your review, feedback, and support will help me to greatly improve my writing craft for future projects and make this book and future books even better.

I wish you all the best in your adventure in hearing God's voice in every area of your life so that you can fulfill the destiny that God has for you.

Please leave your review here: www.amazon.com/dp/B083TC5V8Q or by searching the title on Amazon. Thank you!

ABOUT THE AUTHOR

Rinda Ho is a humble servant of God who is passionate about raising a prophetic generation who loves to fellowship and communicate with the heavenly Father. God has called her to stir and fan the prophetic gift in people as she helps them to activate their five spiritual senses so that they can discern their heavenly Father's voice and to obey His Rhema word for them.

Rinda is a marketplace Christian who is a food technologist by profession. The security of her job that she had for 18 years was suddenly made redundant. She asked God what He wanted her to do. She distinctively heard God say, "My daughter, I want you to write a book." Thus, she became an author who is called by God to write this book. Even the title was given by God.

Rinda loves to coach people and is passionate about sharing how people can connect with God in every area of their lives. She has been invited to various connect groups and churches to activate Christians in hearing God's voice. She has been invited to be a keynote speaker in the Women's Conference as well as teach in various EQUIP classes.

She lives in Perth, Western Australia with her husband and their son and daughter-in-law.

www.ingramcontent.com/pod-product-compliance
Lightning Source LLC
Chambersburg PA
CBHW050309010526
44107CB00055B/2160